Education in Latin America and the Caribbean:
trends and prospects, 1970–2000

Education in Latin America and the Caribbean: trends and prospects, 1970–2000

(Regional Conference of Ministers of Education
and Those Responsible for Economic Planning of
Member States in Latin America and the
Caribbean, organized by Unesco. Mexico City,
1979.)

José Blat Gimeno

unesco

The author is responsible for the choice and the presentation of the facts contained in this book and for the opinions expressed therein, which are not necessarily those of Unesco and do not commit the Organization.

The designations employed and the presentation of material throughout this publication do not imply the expression of any opinion whatsoever on the part of Unesco concerning the legal status of any country, territory, city or area or of its authorities, or concerning the delimitation of its frontiers or boundaries.

Published in 1983 by the United Nations
Educational, Scientific and Cultural Organization
7 place de Fontenoy, 75700 Paris
Printed by Spottiswoode Ballantyne Ltd, Colchester

ISBN 92-3-101908-2
Spanish edition 92-3-301908-X

© Unesco 1983
Printed in the United Kingdom

There are two conflicting views of society and education: one that 'you should knuckle under and resign yourselves to ignorance and poverty'; the other that you should 'achieve material success, even if you have to neglect spiritual considerations'. We have to put young people on their guard against both these views. A civilization that has no culture defrauds the people who sustain it. And a culture deprived of the means of attaining civilization wanes and eventually falls into decay. The choice between technology and the humanities is a false one. We should endeavour to counter it by aiming at both the humanities and technology.

Jaime Torres Bodet

Preface

The purpose of this book is to describe the situation and prospects for education in Latin America and the Caribbean in the light of the discussions and recommendations of the Regional Conference of Ministers of Education and Those Responsible for Economic Planning of Member States in Latin America and the Caribbean which met in Mexico City from 4 to 13 December 1979.[1]

The Conference was organized by Unesco with the co-operation of the United Nations Economic Commission for Latin America (ECLA) and the Organization of American States (OAS). It was attended by twenty-seven delegations from the Member States of Unesco, the Associate Members of Unesco and Territories of the region, by observers from four other Member States and from the Holy See, and by nineteen representatives and observers from institutions of the United Nations system and twenty-nine observers from intergovernmental organizations, from international non-governmental organizations that have consultative relations with Unesco and from various other institutions and foundations.

The conference was attended by Enrique V. Iglesias, Executive Secretary of the United Nations Economic Commission for Latin America (ECLA) and by Gabriel Valdés, Deputy Administrator and Director of the regional office for Latin America and the Caribbean of the United Nations Development Programme (UNDP).

This conference was the latest in a series of regional conferences held in Lima (1956), Santiago de Chile (1962), Buenos Aires (1966) and Caraballeda

---

1. The Conference was attended by representatives of the following Member States, Associate Members and Territories of the region: Argentina, Barbados, Bolivia, Brazil, Chile, Colombia, Costa Rica, Cuba, Dominican Republic, Ecuador, El Salvador, Grenada, Guatemala, Haiti, Honduras, Jamaica, Mexico, Nicaragua, Panama, Paraguay, Peru, Suriname, Trinidad and Tobago, Uruguay, Venezuela, the British Eastern Caribbean Group and the Netherlands Antilles.

(1971). The Lima Conference gave a decisive impetus to the development of primary education in the region. Six years later, the Santiago Conference steered the efforts of those responsible for education towards economic and social development. The participants in the Buenos Aires Conference expressed their serious concern over the need for improvement in the quality of education. The Caraballeda Conference concentrated on reforms in secondary education and the importance of gearing science-and-technology teaching to the demands of development. At the Mexico City Conference, the participants expressed a broad determination to democratize education, stressing, in the words of the Director-General of Unesco, Amadou-Mahtar M'Bow, that there could be no democratization of education 'unless the whole population, including the least privileged groups, participated in its functioning, thus making it serve the interests of the entire community'.

Although the official report of the Mexico City Conference has been published, it was naturally given only limited distribution. But the ideas expressed and the recommendations adopted at the conference deserve wider dissemination, particularly as the effort involved in the implementation of the Mexico City Declaration, which sets forth the broad objectives that future education policies in the region should pursue, calls for the large-scale mobilization of resources and persons.

The author of this volume, José Blat Gimeno, was a member of the group of consultants who assisted Unesco in the preparation of the documents for the conference and in its organization. He took part, as a Unesco official, in the previous four regional conferences, and has served as provincial inspector, central inspector, technical deputy secretary-general and director-general of basic education in the Ministry of Education of his native Spain. He is at present technical adviser to the ministry, following twenty-one years at Unesco. He first served as adviser to the Ministries of Education of Ecuador and Colombia and lecturer in the Escuela Normal Superior in Ecuador and the Universidad Pedagógica in Colombia. He was subsequently the co-ordinator of Unesco's Major Education Project for Latin America and head of Unesco's Regional Office for Education in Latin America. At Unesco Headquarters, he has served as head of the Latin America Division, head of the Co-ordination and Evaluation unit of the Education Sector and Director of the Executive Office of the Director-General of Unesco. His published works include *La situación educativa en América Latina* (Unesco, 1960); *La educación básica en América Latina* (Organization of American States, Washington, D.C., 1962); *Educación y desarollo en América Latina* (Editorial Hachette, Buenos Aires, 1967); *La educación en España; bases para una política educativa*, the white paper that served as a basis for the 1970 educational reform (Ministry of Education and Science, Madrid, 1969; the plan of the work, the preparation of several chapters and the revision of the entire work); *Enciclopedia técnica de la educación* (Editorial Santillana, Madrid, 1970; Volume I dealing with School Organization and Administration, the Psychology of Education, Teaching Techniques and Monitoring and Diagnosis Techniques; editor and reviser of the work); numerous articles on different educational subjects in Unesco publications and in Spanish journals and newspapers; the preparation of working documents for conferences of ministers of education in different regions of the world; and *The Education of Primary and Secondary School Teachers: An International Comparative Study* (Unesco, 1981).

Contents

Introduction

The aim of the Unesco Secretariat in publishing this book is to communicate to professional educators, economic and social planners and the general public the themes considered at the Regional Conference of Ministers of Education and Those Responsible for Economic Planning of Member States in Latin America and the Caribbean (Mexico City, December 1979).

Conferences of ministers of education convened by Unesco are usually called upon to consider educational trends, to take stock of the activities carried out by Member States and by Unesco itself in accordance with the recommendations of the previous conference, to examine specific themes of particular importance in connection with the education systems of the region and to make recommendations for future action related to them.

These conferences afford a highly appropriate framework for the adoption of objectives to be pursued and principles to be observed in undertaking education reforms. Apart from the intellectual implications of their conclusions, they are in certain ways of great practical value. The themes they deal with reflect specific situations and issues in the region in which they are held. They provide an opportunity for a broad exchange of experiences and initiatives. Furthermore, the ministerial rank of the participants, who have decision-making powers in their respective offices, facilitates the implementation of the recommendations made. Some of the principles on which the educational policies of many countries are based today were adopted at these conferences.

The Mexico City Conference considered the following questions: developments in Latin America and the Caribbean since the Venezuela Conference (1971); the major issues and priority areas in educational policies in the 1980s; a number of problems concerning socio-economic and cultural development in Member States in Latin America and the Caribbean; the responsibilities of higher education *vis-à-vis* the requirements of development and the democratization of education; subregional, regional and international co-operation for the development of education in Latin America and the

Caribbean in the context of subregional and regional integration and the new international economic order.

The conference unanimously approved the Mexico City Declaration, which sets forth the broad objectives that the educational policies of the countries of the region should pursue in the immediate future. The conference also adopted a number of recommendations concerning various items on its agenda which provide guidance concerning the strengthening and renewal of the education systems of Latin America and the Caribbean.

Such objectives and aims will only be achieved if they are generally accepted and engage the joint efforts of governments, educators, peoples of the region and, needless to say, the international community. It is hoped that this volume will serve to awaken the interest of all these persons and bodies by publicizing, explaining and commenting upon the resolutions of the conference which, in defining ideals for educational renewal and stating the goals to be pursued, open up new and promising prospects for education in the Latin American and Caribbean countries.

The author of this volume drew up the documentation prepared by the Unesco Secretariat for the conference and the final report of the conference. The work also contains observations and suggestions based partly on the thinking of persons eminent in the education world and partly on the results of experiments in this region or other regions which are likely to contribute to the implementation of the recommendations of the Mexico City Conference.

Part One

Educational trends
between 1960 and 1980

Latin America: unity in diversity

Although it is usual to speak of Latin America as if it were a single entity, it actually embodies many racial and cultural differences. The indigenous inhabitants and the European colonizers have created a rich medley of peoples. There are obvious differences between English-speaking and Spanish-speaking America, and between the countries colonized by the Spanish, Portuguese, British and French. But there are also enormous geographical and political differences within many countries. An America with a predominantly indigenous population is found along the Andean cordillera. The Caribbean islands with their black populations represent a mulatto America. The southern cone of the continent is virtually a European America. Finally, there is a mestizo America extending throughout Mexico and Central America.

Such differences are found in Latin American education as well as in many other aspects of the life, history and culture of Latin America. As Octavio Paz[1] has observed, the fact that ancient beliefs and customs are still in existence beneath Western forms testifies to the vitality of the refined cultures that existed before the Spanish conquest.

This heritage merged with European cultural patterns to form a varied and singularly rich culture. Educational activities were marked by a number of early achievements (the foundation of the *Estudio General de Santo Domingo* was followed by the establishment of the Universities of Mexico and San Marcos de Lima in 1551 and the University of San Francisco Xavier in Bolivia in 1634, whereas Harvard and Yale were founded in 1636 and 1701 respectively). Since independence, education has continued to be extended to wider sectors of the population and not merely to minorities. However, it has also suffered from neglect or from insufficient resources, with the result that very large groups of people have remained illiterate.

Two diametrically opposed attitudes generally dominate any discussion of

1. Octavio Paz, 'A Matter of Life and Death; Aztec Myths and Christian Beliefs in Mexico', *Unesco Courier*, August–September 1977.

the history, the present situation and the future prospects of the region. Some people consider it 'the continent of the future', while others are pessimistic, believing that historical necessity will always prevent the peoples of the region from enjoying prosperity and social justice.

These two views raise an important question, which must be considered first: To what extent and in what respects, if any, may Latin America be regarded as part of the Third World or as an underdeveloped region? Our answer will largely depend on what we mean by development, our criteria for assessing it and the various situations, facts and data that have a bearing upon such criteria. The application of the indicators commonly employed to determine the stage of development—Gross National Product (GNP), income distribution, illiteracy, food consumption level, etc.—will yield one set of results. But the answer will be different if, disregarding these standard criteria, we apply a different scale of values and attach more importance to economic growth than to other factors.

In any event, the diversity of situations throughout this geographically vast region precludes any broad generalizations on its living standards or its stage of development. As the Peruvian, Haya de la Torre, so aptly put it, in Latin America there are several time-scales in the same space. Certain sectors of the population enjoy the living standards, amenities and services of modern civilization, while large numbers live in extremely precarious conditions that are inevitably accompanied by impoverishment, disease and ignorance.

Haya de la Torre's words are true of Latin America. Several periods of history can be observed in the same space. The most refined forms of culture are found a short distance from poverty-stricken urban areas—a phenomenon which frequently occurs as a result of development itself—and from rural areas which are either poorly farmed or under latifundiary ownership (according to Horace, it was the *latifundium* that brought Italy to ruin). Moreover, near at hand are communities which, *mutatis mutandis*, live as prehistoric man did, and are only slightly more advanced in their forms of communal living than the Australian Aborigines. However, we need not go to the vast, fabulous land of Brazil, where distances between the different regions reflect the gigantic scale of the country, which has an area of more than 8 million square kilometres, nor need we travel from São Paulo or Rio de Janeiro, with their imposing skyscrapers and opulent museums, to the harsh, forbidding jungles of Amazonia and the Mato Grosso. Let us consider the example of Panama, a small country with an area of 75,000 square kilometres. It is less than 400 kilometres as the crow flies (a very small distance these days) from houses where genuine Renoirs or first editions of Quevedo, Lope de Vega or Fray Luis de Granada are to be found, to Darién where the Choco Indians lead a primitive existence.

The fact is that both development and underdevelopment must be regarded as relative terms. A country may be underdeveloped in the application of science and technology to the industrial production of consumer goods, which may be desirable as they contribute to a higher standard of living or well-being, or rather, a certain level of comfort. However, if we turn from the practicalities of daily life to the realm of culture, intellectual attainment and art, a different picture emerges. Nicaragua is undeniably in the early stages of development. But can it be forgotten that Rubén Darío, the prime force in the renewal of modern Spanish literature, was born in the Nicaraguan village of Metapa in the nineteenth century? In fact, today, in Paris, London, New York and Rome, any list of great literary names whose spirit reflects the finest qualities of western civilization at its highest will include Borges, Jorge Amado, Cortázar, Carlos Fuentes and García Márquez, citizens of what we refer to as developing countries.

The terms 'development' and 'underdevelopment' must, therefore, be used with some caution. Fundamentally, we have to consider the world-view of the different peoples concerned and, consequently, the values that reflect it. Some civilizations endeavour to put knowledge and scientific and technological discovery to immediate, practical use and to turn them to their economic advantage.

In the case of Latin America, the concurrence of several levels of development in a single period of time requires the observer to revise his terminology and refine his ideas. Relativity applies not merely to judgements on macrocosmic phenomena but to the appraisal of the most complex facts of human history.

The concepts of development and underdevelopment cannot be applied mechanically or automatically. It has to be borne in mind that under-development in terms of modern facilities and technological instruments of production does not necessarily imply underdevelopment in terms of all the spiritual phenomena, the flower of civilizations and the crown of history, which we call culture.

One recent phenomenon augurs exceedingly well for the future of the region. In the Caribbean and the vast region of Latin America, newly independent nations have added their voices to the great chorus expressing the determination of those who are aware that the world can find a solution to its problems in the vast field of education, science and culture.

The great transformation, which began in the nineteenth century and became more widespread as the century drew to a close, is now nearing completion as the peoples of the region come to maturity. Newly independent states bring to the common heritage of the region new characteristics which reflect their diverse origins and the ways in which they have attained modernity. While some of them are small in geographical and population terms, these new countries have been received in the region in a brotherly spirit and have been accepted as fully fledged historical entities. For it should be said, in the light of the lessons of classical antiquity, that there is no country that cannot be great even though it is small, no people that cannot attain nation-hood. It is precisely in the United Nations system—and particularly in Unesco by reason of its purpose and ideals—that the principle of the equality of states, which is the cornerstone of international law, is fully acknowledged and observed.

It is really a question of cultural personalities. The Member States of

Unesco are the champions of a new culture, a new humanism, which will make this region the homeland of mankind, a land where there is no room for racial, religious or ideological distinctions. However, this new culture does not imply uniformity or the creation of a vast, monotonous and dull world. This planetary culture, which is coming into being through progress in all aspects of life, and particularly in technology, will lead to an accentuation of stylistic differences rather than monotony or repetition. While all these countries have common instruments and aims—well-being, democracy, education, science and culture—each employs these instruments and pursues these aims according to its own particular style and its own personality which is shaped by its historical heritage and its ecosociological conditions.

The Caribbean area, therefore, enriches the cultures of the region by making a cultural contribution that is both diverse and extremely valuable. However, this cultural multiplicity does not detract from the force of such powerful ties as the use of a common language by twenty countries, as well as the values and traits that give the peoples of Latin America and the Caribbean their own distinctive appearance.

This thought is expressed in language of great poetic beauty and of immense value in human and, particularly, 'anti-racist' terms, by Lope de Vega, the great sixteenth-century Spanish dramatist, when he states that Spaniards differ from American blacks and mulattos only in the fact that 'a stronger sun shines on them on our common road to death'.[1] The efforts being made today to achieve development are characterized by common problems, aspirations and trends that originate in historical factors, external influences and aims that are shared by all. It is not for nothing that people in the region speak of 'integration' in two senses: that of the self-assertion of the region as such and its presence on the world scene, and that of co-operation between countries with a view to meeting their common needs. The climate of understanding and the consensus achieved at the Mexico City Conference are an expression of this principle of unity or of determination to achieve it. As Leopoldo Zea states:

The Ibero-American peoples cannot, at this stage, follow the path of western peoples, for they are late comers to the western world; but they can be a great community, the Iberian community, which sees that its own interests are respected without disregarding those of other peoples. As Bolivar realized, unless the Ibero-American peoples unite, they will never do more than provide grazing lands for those peoples who have made their own material growth and the enrichment of their citizens one of the main goals of their expansion.[2]

1. Félix Lope de Vega y Carpio, *La Dragontea*.
2. Leopoldo Zea, *América en la historia*, Mexico City, Fondo de Cultura Económica, 1957.

Educational trends and the conferences of ministers of the region

The Lima Conference (1956)

The year 1956 was a significant one for Latin American education: it marked the beginning of a wide-ranging series of activities at international and regional levels, aimed at providing support and aid for national policies and measures in the field of education. The Regional Conference on Free and Compulsory Education in Latin America was held in Lima in late April and early May of that year.

The Lima Conference was the first of the meetings convened by Unesco as part of a programme of worldwide action aimed, first, at giving an impetus to the development of primary education and, subsequently, at spreading the idea that educational planning should be related to economic and social development in the different parts of the world. (The corresponding conferences in other parts of the world are the Karachi Conference in 1960 and the Addis Ababa Conference in 1961.)

The themes studied by the Regional Conference were considered by a large number of top-level educational administrators and specialists from different countries and various international agencies. This was possible since the conference met at practically the same time as three other major meetings held in Lima: the second Inter-American Meeting of Ministers of Education (convened by the OAS, 3–9 May 1956), the second Meeting of the Inter-American Cultural Council (3–12 May 1956) and the Seminar on Primary Education Syllabuses and Curricula for Latin America (Huampaní, Lima, 9–22 May 1956). An exhaustive and—most important of all—a highly objective study of primary education problems in Latin America was made for the first time in Lima. It drew attention to the effects of educational backwardness on the economic development of the countries in the region. The conference pointed out that plans for the development of primary education (using modern planning techniques) should be drawn up, and recommended that such plans be co-ordinated with social and economic development plans. With a view to facilitating the implementation of this recommendation, the conference pointed out the desirability of establishing national commissions for educational planning, and stressed the pressing need to set up national statistics services, which it viewed as a prerequisite to good planning.

The main recommendations adopted on the subject of the extension of primary education included one to the effect that free and compulsory primary education should be provided for at least six years and another stipulating that the education provided in urban schools and rural schools should be of the same duration and quality.

These recommendations were repeated at subsequent conferences (Santiago, 1962, and Buenos Aires, 1966). The activities planned in connection with Unesco's first Major Project (see below) played an important part in their gradual implementation. The principles of these two recommendations are now accepted in the region. However, in large areas of Latin America, there are still many schools, particularly rural schools, which do not provide the complete primary course. On the other hand, the duration of basic general education has been extended to eight or nine years in some countries. This trend is gradually becoming more widespread.

The Major Project on the Extension and Improvement of Primary Education in Latin America

The resolution which was to have the greatest impact on Latin American education was that which approved in principle a ten-year 'major project' aimed at the extension and improvement of primary education in Latin America. It was adopted a few months later by the General Conference of Unesco meeting in New Delhi in November and December 1956. The Conference incorporated the project into the programme and budget of Unesco. The project was begun in mid-1957 and was completed in 1966. Since the Mexico City Conference (1979) recommended the adoption of another major project, we shall say something of the first such project in the region. Apart from the historical interest of the approach adopted and the results achieved in the earlier project, the experience gained in its execution may prove useful to those planning the new project.

The aims of the Major Project were as follows:

1. To encourage systematic educational planning in the Latin American countries.
2. To further the extension of primary education services through continued large-scale efforts during the course of the project, with a view to achieving the objective of providing adequate educational coverage for the school-age population of Latin America by 1968.
3. To give an impetus to the revision of primary school syllabuses and curricula so that they should offer all children equal educational opportunities in terms of the duration of schooling and the level of education, be adapted effectively to the particular needs of the population

in the different areas or regions of each country and reflect the new approaches which social changes and the aspirations of society demand from education.

4. To bring about improvements in teacher-training systems, to give an impetus to the provision of regular in-service training for teachers, and to contribute to efforts to raise the economic and social status of the teaching profession.

5. To prepare, for each Latin American country, a nucleus of top education administrators and specialists, with a university or equivalent training, who will be capable of steering and giving momentum to the reforms and advances needed in primary education in Latin America.

Organization and administration

The Intergovernmental Advisory Committee

This committee was set up to advise the Director-General of Unesco on all questions concerning the preparation and implementation of the Major Project which he might require it to consider. It was initially composed of the representatives of twelve countries, and was subsequently enlarged to include representatives of all the countries of the region (1962).

During the course of the project, the Advisory Committee held six meetings to examine the two-year work plans, evaluate completed activities and propose lines of action which, if reflected in Unesco and government policies, would make it possible to ensure the necessary regional co-ordination in each of the countries with a view to attaining the aims and targets of the project.

The national commissions for Unesco

The national commissions disseminated information among the public and participated in the allocation of fellowships. In some countries, they organized working committees in connection with the Major Project.

The co-ordination office for the Major Project

The co-ordinator of the Major Project was directly responsible for its administration, under the supervision and guidance of the director of Unesco's Department of Education. The office of the co-ordinator was initially located in Havana and moved to Santiago in 1961. Curriculum specialists, experts in statistics and planning and travelling experts made their services available to this office.

Associated normal schools

Five normal schools in Colombia, Ecuador, Honduras and Nicaragua associated themselves with the project; they received technical co-operation, equipment and documentation from Unesco, in connection with the fourth objective of the project. In general, they served as pilot centres with the aim of improving teacher-training curricula in the countries of the region, training unqualified teachers, providing in-service training for teachers and preparing administrators, inspectors and principals. It was hoped that their experiences, organization and methods would help to bring about the progressive improvement of national systems of initial and further training for teachers.

Associated universities

Two universities—the University of São Paulo (Brazil) and the University of Chile—associated themselves with the Major Project with a view to contributing to the attainment of its fifth objective. The University of São Paulo introduced a course to train education specialists for Latin America. In conjunction with the Chilean Ministry of Education, the University of Chile established the Latin American Centre for the Training of Education Specialists.

In addition to the specialist training work of these centres, mention should also be made of the activities connected with the initial and further training course for teachers at the University of La Plata in Argentina and the activities of the Regional Centre for Adult Education and Functional Literacy for Latin America (CREFAL) (Mexico) and IAREC (Venezuela). The educators of the region were able to benefit from these activities owing to a programme of scholarships funded by Unesco and by other agencies and countries co-operating in the project.

Publications programme

The publications programme proved to be one of the most effective ways of reinforcing the activities of the training courses and seminars and the technical advisory services provided by travelling experts in the different countries. A number of monographs and manuals were published, and a quarterly bulletin was widely distributed in the region. In several cases, these and other Unesco publications formed the nucleus of new education libraries and educational documentation centres.

The main achievements

The Major Project gave an impetus to regional action and demonstrated the scale and nature of educational problems in Latin America, thereby arousing considerable public interest.

The Major Project did much to promote the extension of primary education in Latin America. Between 1957 and 1965, enrolments in primary education went up by 11,679,622, rising from 21,235,455 to 32,915,077. This means that enrolments rose by more than 50 per cent in this period, and the annual increase was more than 5.1 per cent, a greater increase than the population growth-rate, which was approximately 2.8 per cent a year. The number of primary-school teachers increased from 634,000 to almost a million, and the number of unqualified teachers fell. The number of schools and school buildings went up proportionally with the increase in enrolments and in the number of teachers. The number of teacher-training establishments, trainee teachers and newly trained teachers also increased. In most countries, the percentage of the national budget earmarked for education rose (the average rise was from 13.3 to 16.6 per cent). There was an improvement in educational efficiency (in 1957, 19 per cent of those pupils who had enrolled in the first year completed the course successfully; by 1965, this figure had risen to 23 per cent).

The Major Project concentrated primarily on teacher education, and helped to clarify ideas about the type of teacher needed in Latin America. In addition to this theoretical contribution, the experience of the associated centres served as a point of reference for the reforms in teacher education undertaken in the region. The Associated Normal Schools and other pilot centres organized with the co-operation of Unesco helped to improve the quality of the national teacher-training systems in the countries in which they operated, through their experimental work with syllabuses, curricula, methods and new forms of organization.

Encouraging results were achieved in the provision of training for top educational administrators and education specialists. More than 1,652 fellowship-holders took courses in school inspection, teacher education, educational and vocational guidance and syllabus and curriculum preparation. Most of them held responsible positions in educational administration or in teaching. In this way the initial aim of the project was achieved: to train small nuclei of specialized personnel in each Latin American country, who could give an impetus to eductaion and improve its quality.

Special mention should be made of the work done in the comprehensive planning of education, which was added to the project's objectives in 1958. Ten years later, almost all the ministries of education, several universities and a number of central economic planning bureaux had educational planning services. These services succeeded in providing an accurate, all-round view of educational needs and in forecasting the nature and scale of the efforts that would be required in the future. The courses arranged at the Latin American Institute for Economic and Social Planning (ILPES) from 1962 on were attended by some 200 fellowship-holders, who subsequently worked in the planning services of their respective countries or in other posts in the ministries of education.

The Major Project was an object lesson in the organization of an education plan. It was based on a guiding principle and a number of specific objectives which were methodically achieved. This showed what could be done by joint action at regional level. It was also proof of the existence of international solidarity, which was reflected in the fact that various international agencies and centres, American and European countries, universities, etc., co-operated in the implementation of the project.

The tangible achievements of the project were complemented by a less conspicuous yet extremely significant factor which made a considerable contribution to the development of education in the region: the interest in education shown by different groups in society, particularly the family; the socio-economic groups concerned now have a clearer idea of how an effective education system could contribute to the expansion of economic development in the countries of the region. This change of attitude towards educational problems, which holds out so much promise for the future, was brought about in particular by the persistent efforts of both Unesco and the ministries of education to influence public opinion.

The Major Project soon went beyond the limits of teacher education for primary teachers; it served as a focal point for Latin American public interest in educational problems and the relationship between education and development, and threw light on these matters. Moreover, it gave people in each country a better knowledge of the achievements of other countries in the field of education. In this way, it stimulated a healthy rivalry, and to a considerable extent it enabled educational problems to be seen in a regional perspective.

The project made a major contribution to education by bringing about improvements in school statistics, particularly in regard to the analysis and comparability of such statistics as essential instruments in the assessment of the situation of educational services and the planning of their future development. Other major contributions were the training of education specialists technically qualified to undertake, in their respective countries, the study of educational problems as a basis for the formulation of effective policies, and the rapid dissemination of the principles and methods of all-round educational planning. Practically all Latin American countries established educational planning services. Apart from the extraordinary increase in the number of students, this was undoubtedly the most significant way in which the Major Project influenced education policy in Latin American countries.

Although the primary aim of the Major Project was the expansion of education services, it was constantly concerned with improving the quality of these services, since it took as its starting-point the assumption that educational planning and educational reform are distinct yet inseparable processes. Another fundamental aspect in which a positive change of attitude is to be seen is the conception of the unity of the education process and the way in which this unity should be reflected in the structure of the school system.

There has also been an important change in the concept of rural education, and expectations in regard to literacy campaigns or programmes have become more realistic. There is now a readiness to recognize that educational opportunities should be of comparable quality in the cities and in the countryside. Literacy campaigns are seen in the broader context of social action, and greater importance is attached to the techniques involved in the organization of such campaigns.

The vast amount of literature produced in connection with the project was fully used by the teacher-training and other specialist-training establishments in studying the educational problems of the region.

In short, it may be said that the Major Project helped to bring about the marked changes that have taken place in the education policies of Latin American countries, and that these changes were reflected in the noteworthy development of their school services, and in more careful and more dynamic planning to solve the problems that will have to be dealt with in the future.

The Santiago Conference (1962)

For a variety of reasons, this conference gave a great impetus, in both theoretical and practical terms, to the development of the lines of emphasis, priorities and forms of action to be pursued in education policies in the region. For one thing, this was the first meeting of the ministers of education and those responsible for economic planning; for another, the countries of Latin America were going through a period when expectations in relation to political and social changes were high, and it was hoped that economic development, accelerated as a result of the national effort and international co-operation, would make it possible to improve the living standards and living conditions of their people; and the joint support of the General Conference of Unesco, the United Nations Economic Commission for Latin America (ECLA) and the OAS made it possible to provide technical documentation in which education plans were integrated with economic and social development plans with a more than usual degree of success.

The conference made it clear what the role of education was as a factor of development and as a form of investment, what its function was in relation to the demand for professional personnel, and what its task was as a mechanism of social change, a means of selection and social advancement and an instrument of technical progress.

The Declaration of Santiago, approved by the conference, reaffirmed the commitments undertaken in the United Nations Charter, the Unesco Constitution, the Charter of the Organization of American States and the Punta del Este Charter in the field of education, and affirmed that it was a matter of the utmost urgency that priority should be given to international co-operation in the promotion of education in Latin America.

Among other things, the Conference recommended:

that... steps be taken... to formulate educational development programmes integrated with overall economic and social development plans which, without neglecting the all-round education of the human person, establish suitable priorities for increasing the people's productivity so as to accelerate the economic and social advancement of the whole population;

that each and every one of the States... take the necessary steps to devote to education the maximum economic resources compatible with its productive and financial capacity and with the balance of other social costs, so as to achieve in 1965 a situation in which Latin America as a whole can devote to education not less than 4 per cent of its gross product;

that Unesco explore the possibility of establishing an International Fund for Education in Latin America and that, pending the achievement of this aim, it invite all the States that are members of the organizations in the United Nations system to make contributions for the purpose of increasing the resources of the international financing agencies concerned, so that they may give effective support to the efforts undertaken by the Latin American countries.

The plan of action was presented in very broad terms so that it could be easily adapted to conditions in each country. It covered the following aspects.

Structure and administration of educational services

The principles on which the recommendations were based included: (a) the maximum use of the available resources; (b) a structure geared to the provision of a general education of the longest possible duration; (c) the adoption of measures designed to ensure equal opportunities of access to education; (d) the integration of services responsible for educational research, school buildings, the production of textbooks and teaching materials and school libraries into the education services; (e) the rationalization of the education services and the introduction of technology into them; (f) the decentralization of authority; (g) the restructuring of school inspection services and the adoption of new aims for them; and (h) the evaluation of school efficiency, in both quantitative and qualitative terms, in such a way as to relate the financial and human resources earmarked for education to their efficiency.

Primary education

Generally speaking, the conference reaffirmed the principles on which the recommendations of the Lima Conferences (1956) were based, particularly in regard to equal opportunities for access to education, school survival rate, equality in terms of the duration and quality of the education provided in urban and rural areas, and the training, further training and status of teachers.

For the first time acceptable minima were specified for the duration of school education: the school year was to consist of not less than 200 school days; the school day was to be of not less than five hours' duration. Although the countries of the region made considerable efforts to achieve these targets, in many of them the limited amount or inadequate use of resources and the enormous increase in the demand for education led to a deterioration rather than an improvement in the situation.

Secondary education

While recognizing the importance of according priority to the extension of primary education to all, the recommendations advocated that efforts be stepped up to bring about the progressive extension, particularly the first phase, of secondary education to all, in accordance with the principle of providing a general education of the longest possible duration.

Generally speaking, the recommendations were based on the principles of co-ordination between the different levels of education, the correlation of subjects, the flexibility of syllabuses, and the selection of curriculum content on the basis of the extent to which it enables the pupil to study by himself, develops a critical attitude in him and strengthens his character.

Higher education

The main recommendations concerned inter-university co-operation, the teacher-training course in institutions of higher education, the trial introduction of new forms of higher education which would allow better use of resources and would more effectively help to meet the need for middle-level personnel created by economic developments and the role of the universities in training the scientists and technicians required to speed up the process of social and economic change, on the basis of an evaluation of the nation's need for specialized graduate personnel.

Technical and vocational education

The conference called attention to the fact that vocational training should be provided as part of an education plan that is in line with a national policy of economic and social development designed to raise the living standard through the optimum use of all the human resources of the country. It also adopted a series of recommendations concerning the better use of resources, the need for a knowledge of the manpower and employment situation, the role of educational and vocational guidance schemes, the desirability of establishing training services outside the normal phases of education, which are associated with enterprises and labour organizations of all kinds, and the training, further training and status of teachers.

In addition to these theoretical recommendations, the conference formulated various guidelines and recommendations of a practical nature. One of these recommendations led directly to the systematic activities aimed at training educational planning specialists undertaken by Unesco in co-operation with ILPES.

To conclude this survey of the conference, it should be noted that the dialogue that took place at it between educators, economists and sociologists laid the foundations for collaboration which has continued until the present day. This collaboration has done much to make people realize that the education system should be regarded not as an independent system which is cut off from society at large, but as an essential part of society which, while in some way reflecting social characteristics, is at the same time a powerful instrument for achieving social development, bringing about far-reaching changes and promoting the advancement of peoples.

The Buenos Aires Conference (1966)

Unlike the Santiago Conference, which was held when conditions were favourable, the Buenos Aires Conference met under adverse circumstances, which affected its proceedings and even led to its premature termination. The political instability that plagues many countries of the region was exemplified by the fact that the President of the Republic, who had personally taken part in the inauguration ceremony, had left office before the end of the conference and before the end of his mandate under the Argentine Constitution. The political tensions between a number of countries at that time were hardly conducive to the calm, congenial atmosphere so essential to a conference of this kind. These difficulties were compounded by an unexpected period of heavy rain which made the conference building unusable.

All this made it impossible to devote the necessary time and attention to a theme of such importance as the completion of the Major Project on the extension and improvement of primary education, or to consider, as a number of delegations wished, the possibility of continuing the project for the other phases of education. To do so would have been both logical and desirable, particularly as the considerable impetus given to the expansion of primary education by the Major Project had led to a heavy increase in the demand for school places in the different stages and types of secondary education.

The conference recommended that each country should decide its educational policy on the following lines:

An effort should be made to maintain the high rates of expansion in education in order to reinforce what has been achieved during the last decade, ensure harmonious and balanced development at all levels and in all branches, eliminate the anomalies in the education pyramid—in particular by improving retention rates—and provide for the training of the cadres required for economic and social development.

More should be done to improve the quality of education by taking action in regard to the training and continuing in-service training of teachers, the content of teaching and its methods, the utilization of the resources which modern technology offers—thereby making it possible to extend the benefits of education—and educational research.

An attempt should be made to involve the university more fully in the national planning of education as a whole and of development.

Favourable attitudes should be cultivated with a view to helping achieve the cultural and economic integration towards which the countries of the region are striving.

An appropriate rate of increase in the financial resources allocated to education should be maintained, their distribution being made in proportion to the needs at each level and in each educational sector, and efforts should be made to ensure that they are put to the best use.

In regard to 'human resources', the conference made a series of recommendations to the governments and international agencies to the effect that studies should be undertaken of the problems arising from the relationships between education, employment, the labour market, national development plans and the career choice of the individual.

In regard to the structure of education systems, the conference reaffirmed the principles of the unity of the education process and of flexibility and co-ordination between the various phases and forms of education, which had been stated in Lima and Santiago. It also proposed the following general pattern: a pre-school course, a common general phase lasting eight to nine years, a second phase divided into different branches of education and a higher-education level comprising, besides the traditional courses, new specialized studies and short courses, as well as such post-graduate courses as the employment structure may require.

On the subject of educational administration, the conference recommended the rationalization of services, the decentralization of administration, the delegation of responsibilities and the modernization of the ancillary administration services (with special attention given to educational statistics services) and supervision.

The theme of 'general and specialized education' evoked the reaffirmation of the principles that the all-round development of man called for a balance between general and specialized education, and that general education should be as comprehensive as possible and of the longest possible duration. The conference also set out the basic content of general education and the essential points to be covered in all specialized training plans. The conference recommended that priority should be given to technical and vocational education in national education policies.

In regard to the training of personnel, the conference noted the recommendations of previous meetings and introduced a number of new points. It recommended that, in those countries where the structure of secondary education had been remodelled on the basis of a common phase of general education, teacher-training schools should devote themselves entirely to professional training; it also pointed out the desirability of training a new type of primary-school teacher, specializing in allied subjects, who would teach in an intermediate phase between the basic phase of general education and the differentiated phase of secondary education.

The Venezuela Conference (1971)

The Venezuela Conference, held in December 1971, was the first conference in the region for which invitations were extended both to ministers of education and to those responsible for the promotion of science and technology in relation to development. The major themes of the conference were the democratization and renewal of the education systems, the reform of secondary education, the teaching of science and technology, and Latin American integration.

The conference thoroughly examined the question of the democratization of education and pointed out that equality of educational opportunity implies not merely access to education but the possibility of successfully completing it. In this connection, the conference recommended a broad series of measures including the provision of special educational assistance for children whose deprived socio-cultural background puts them at a disadvantage in relation to children from more privileged social groups, and the introduction of educational standards, drop-out classes and individualized instruction with a view to preventing any further rise in the number of repeaters. The conference went on to advocate the reform of excessively rigid educational structures which hamper the continuity and diversification of the different phases and forms of education. It also stressed the need to co-ordinate school and out-of-school activities.

On the subject of secondary-school education, the conference recommended increasing the number of branches of education and specializations, the introduction of work-experience activities and the establishment of secondary schools in rural areas. With a view to the modernization of science and technology teaching, the conference suggested the introduction of exchanges of personnel specializing in the provision of further training for science and technology teachers, and greater efforts to furnish instructional materials and literature in this area of educational renewal. The conference also advocated the institutionalization of out-of-school scientific activities and the organization of permanent competitions and exhibitions in science and technology. In short, it took the view that this broad range of activities, directed towards the improvement of science-and-technology teaching, was both an essential aspect of any effort to raise the level of efficiency and the quality of the education system and the primary driving-force behind the acceleration of economic and social development.

On the question of Latin American integration, the delegates were unanimous in their view that Latin American unity should not be regarded as abstract uniformity, but should be based on recognition of the specific diversity of cultures and situations. With the aim of promoting action directed towards integration, the conference expressed the view that Unesco should co-operate with subregional agencies set up by countries in the same geographical area and projects of interest to certain groups of countries, even though they are not necessarily situated in the same subregional area. In this context, the conference defined the lines of activity to be pursued by each of Unesco's regional offices in Latin America and the Caribbean. It is interesting to note that the Conference of Ministers, eager to ensure the effective implementation of its recommendations, adopted a resolution (subsequently ratified by the General Conference of Unesco) to conduct a periodic evaluation of all the activities undertaken in this connection by Unesco and the Latin American and Caribbean countries. In accordance with this resolution, Unesco organized a meeting of the representatives of the ministries of education of the region. This meeting was held in Panama in February 1976.

Conclusions

Today, a number of conclusions may be drawn regarding the extent of the effective implementation of the objectives and guidelines laid down at the successive conferences of ministers of education and those responsible for economic planning or for the promotion of science and technology. Not all of these conclusions are favourable.

First, it seems fairly certain, particularly in the case of the first two of these conferences, that hopes regarding the actual power of education were set too high. This is nothing new: since the age of the Enlightenment in particular, people have expressed optimism and confidence about the effects of education which have not been borne out by the facts.

For example, the main objective of the Lima Conference, which gave the name to the Major Project—the extension and improvement of primary education—was not attained. Despite the considerable achievements in this field, the target of full enrolment of school-age children had not been met at the end of the decade spanned by the project.

More than twenty years later, in 1979, the Mexico City Conference adopted a similar objective. The approach was more realistic, but more ambitious in the sense that a ten-year period of school education was set as a target, although it was not expected to be realized until the year 2000. This does not detract from the merits of the Major Project which, as we have seen, produced highly significant results in terms of improving the quality of primary education and in the training systems for primary school teachers and education specialists. Moreover, the increases in the expansion of primary education brought about by the Major Project were by no means negligible.

The Santiago Conference gave a great impetus to the dissemination of new ideas and principles regarding the relationship between educational action and economic and social development. However, the expectations to which it gave rise did not fully materialize. In Latin America, as in other regions of the world, assumptions and ideas that were accepted without question at that time are now being revised. Although the education systems now do more to train young people for work, and have provided them with new vocational opportunities, the economic crisis and the disparities between employment prospects, types of occupation and work for trainees have frustrated these efforts and led to unemployment. This has weakened the widely held belief that occupational training would create new job opportunities by its own momentum. Education itself cannot ensure employment. The dynamic of the job market is primarily affected by the pace and nature of economic growth and the degree to which socio-economic structures are changed. None the less, it is equally certain that people's desire to play a productive part in the labour force and generate income and their ability to do so are largely determined by their level of education and their job qualifications. While education can help them in this way, with varying degrees of success and efficiency, it can also, from time to time, make unemployment and underemployment worse.

If education is to be related to employment, national development must be seen and planned as a whole, so that economic, employment and manpower-training targets are co-ordinated in such a way as to minimize inconsistencies and anomalies which may be produced either by the failure of the economic system to provide employment for those who are being educated or by the fact that the structure, growth dynamics and content of the education provided are unrelated to the realities and changing requirements of the world of work.

The convergence of both these factors in the region has given rise to mounting concern about the problems resulting from this relationship. In recent years, concern has grown in view of the difficulties experienced by some school-leavers and graduates in finding jobs, unemployment among technicians and professional people, with the consequent brain drain, and underemployment due to the lack of jobs suited to the level of people's education and expectations. In the 1950s and 1960s and for most of the 1970s, it was believed that a comprehensive development policy, geared to general economic growth, would almost automatically solve the employment problem,

at least to a large degree. Subsequent events have shown the erroneous nature
and serious consequences of such an assumption. The employment problem
worsened in the 1960s when the unemployment and underemployment figures
became one of the major indicators of the stagnation and structural inefficiency
of the economies of the region. With a high population growth, the overall rate
of unemployment rose from 5.6 to 11.1 per cent between 1950 and 1965. This
increase brought the total number of unemployed in the region as a whole to 9
million.

This factor has, logically enough, hampered the achievement of another of
the goals stated at the Santiago Conference, that of accelerating mobility and
furthering social advancement through education, particularly vocational
education.

Should we be pessimistic about the validity of the principles embraced at
these conferences, about their realism or about the shortcomings or
inadequacies in their implementation? The answer to this threefold question
is simple: the spirit which inspired these principles is undiminished and
enduring, in so far as the purpose of development was seen as the creation of
a more just and prosperous society. The imbalances and inadequacies
encountered in vocational training are not merely a result of the state of the
educational system. They are also due to the fact that such training has not
always been accompanied by social action on the part of the state designed to
create new industries and types of occupation and, consequently, new jobs.

In any event, the period of twenty years which has elapsed since the first of
these conferences is not long enough for any definitive conclusions to be
reached concerning the effects of education, whose nature is such that they can
only be seen in the long term. Even if we take the most pessimistic view of the
situation, it is obvious that, on balance, the results are very favourable and
even encouraging. These results are: (a) the considerable expansion of the
education systems; (b) the raising of the average level of education of the
population; and (c) the significant increase in the number of professionals and
trained personnel able to undertake a variety of occupations as a result of
receiving a general education, which eliminates the disadvantages experienced
by illiterates in this respect.

These factors are further confirmation of the fact that education plans will
only be wholly effective if they are preceded or accompanied by political, social
and economic action aimed at development and the necessary social changes. It
can be said that the opposite has in fact occurred, that is to say, the reforms and
the expansion of education systems have preceded economic development
plans.

The expansion of the education system: developments, trends and problems[1]

The overall situation

In Latin America, interest in education began to grow in the early 1950s. Since the dawn of Latin American independence, outstanding leaders and groups of intellectuals had endeavoured to further both the education of élites and education of the people at large. In the early part of this century, action was taken by certain political movements. But the results achieved fell short of what was hoped. A very large proportion of the population was untouched by their efforts and received no education. This situation was also in some degree due to the apprehensions of certain political and economic pressure groups about the general extension of education and culture, which they saw as a potential threat to their interests and privileges. Education was also hampered by the fact that extremely limited budgetary resources were made available for it.

Attitudes towards education changed in the family, in society at large and among the authorities. Individual families became aware of the value of education as a means of financial betterment and social ascent, and wanted their children to enjoy such opportunities. At a collective level, large sectors of Latin American society turned to education as one of the ways of securing emancipation from their precarious or intolerable living conditions. Economic planners saw the new outlook in education as a means of creating wealth; when presenting government programmes, political leaders would frequently refer to educational objectives and plans. The intellectual work done and the technical assistance provided by international agencies, and Unesco in particular, met with valuable co-operation from the United Nations Economic Commission for Latin America. These agencies also drew up plans for co-

1. The data contained in this chapter are taken from the documents *Education in the Context of Development in Latin America and the Caribbean* (ED-79/MINEDLAC/3) and *Quantitative Evolution Projections of Enrolment in the Educational Systems of Latin America and the Caribbean. Statistical Analysis* (ED-79/MINEDLAC/Ref. 2), prepared by the Unesco Secretariat for the Mexico City Conference, 4–13 December 1979.

operation with the OAS and provided guidance and support for the national efforts which took their origin and momentum from this new attitude favouring the development of education systems.

Results were achieved within a very short time. The years 1950 to 1960 were characterized by a significant average annual rate of increase in primary-education enrolments. In the 1960s, expansion was faster in secondary education, while in the 1970s growth in higher education was proportionately greater than in other levels of education. These growth trends are illustrated in Table 1.

TABLE 1. Enrolment by level of education in the region (in thousands), both sexes, 1960–1970

Level of education	1960	1965	1970	1975	1977	Absolute average annual increases			1977 growth index 1960 = 100
						1960–65	1965–70	1970–77	
First	27 095	35 718[1]	46 538	56 412	60 315	1 725	2 164	1 968	223
Second	2 833	4 724	7 352	12 134	14 076	378	526	961	497
Third	546	871	1 573	3 513	4 267	65	140	385	782
TOTAL	30 474	41 313	55 463	72 059	78 658	2 168	2 830	3 314	258

1. The difference between the figure referring to enrolment in primary education in 1965 and the figure given in the paragraph referring to the results achieved through the Major Project is due to the fact that the figures in this table correspond, in the case of Brazil and Chile, to the new structures providing for eight grades of basic education.
Source: Quantitative Evolution Projections of Enrolment in the Educational Systems of Latin America and the Caribbean. Statistical Analysis (ED-79/MINEDLAC/Ref. 2), prepared by the Unesco Secretariat for the Conference of Ministers of Education held in Mexico City, 4–13 December 1979.

The growth in total enrolment between 1960 and 1977 was consistently higher than that of the population (aged 6 to 23) corresponding to the most common ages for enrolment. The average annual growth rate for this period was 5.7 per cent, which was twice as high as the growth rate of the population in this age-bracket. Between 1960 and 1977, the total number of enrolments in primary, secondary and higher education rose from 30.5 million to 78.7 million, representing an absolute increase of 48.2 million. This increase was distributed as follows: 33.2 million enrolments in primary education, 11.3 million in secondary education and 3.8 million in higher education. In relative terms, the rates of increase over the 1960–77 period were 681.5 per cent in higher education, 396.9 per cent in secondary education and 122.6 per cent in primary education. The lower growth rate in primary education is largely due to school attendance reaching saturation levels in various countries of the region.

Educational progress in the region in terms of coverage can be better assessed by looking at the school-enrolment ratios by age-groups. In 1960, formal education systems covered 57.6 per cent of the population between the ages of 6 and 11, 35.9 per cent of the 12–17 age-group and 6.2 per cent of the 18–23 age-group. By 1977, these figures had risen to 78.7, 60.2 and 22.1 per cent respectively.

The pace at which Member States in the region have extended school enrolment in this decade has varied considerably. While in some countries total enrolment grew at an average annual rate of 6 per cent or more, others have failed to attain an average of 2 per cent.

In 1976, general education still represented the main element (70.5 per cent) in secondary-school enrolment. In trade, technical and vocational education as a whole, the commercial branch accounted for over 50 per cent of enrolments, and industrial education for over 26 per cent.

The gross rate of transition from secondary to higher education has increased considerably (from about 24 per cent in 1966 to about 34 per cent in 1975, with variations ranging from 5.9 per cent in Trinidad and Tobago to 65.5 per cent in Bolivia). In 1975, the gross secondary-school-enrolment ratios in these two countries were 39.4 and 27.4 per cent respectively.

With the exception of a few countries, school enrolment in rural areas has gradually declined in relation to the total student body, mainly because of the drift from the country to the cities. In some countries, the annual rate of increase in enrolments over the last fifteen years has been extremely low or even negative. In others, it has topped 5 per cent. None the less, growth has kept up in absolute terms. In the early 1960s, rural primary-school enrolments in the region amounted to 8.8 million pupils. By 1975, the figure was 20.4 million. These figures represent 41.3 and 36.4 per cent respectively of total primary-school enrolments for those years. In 1960, for every 100 rural primary pupils, there were 143 urban pupils at the same level. This ratio rose to 148 in 1965 and to 175 in 1975. If rural enrolment figures are compared with the total school population, i.e. students at all levels of education, the relative decline becomes even steeper. In 1960, rural enrolments represented 34.2 per cent of the total number of students in the region. This figure had fallen to 24.9 per cent by 1975.

Female enrolment has been expanding very rapidly throughout the region. At primary and secondary levels, regional analysis of the comparative situation is pointless, since the participation of the sexes in education is virtually equal. Women represented 29 per cent of the total enrolments in higher education up to 1960. By 1977, this figure had risen to 42 per cent. The total number of women students in higher education increased elevenfold between 1960 and 1977 and has trebled since 1970. Between 1960 and 1977, the average annual rate of increase in female enrolment in the region was 15.3 per cent.

Between 1970 and 1976, enrolments in the public and private educational subsystems expanded at different rates. While regional enrolment in public education increased at an average rate of 5.4 per cent, the figure for private education was 6.2 per cent. It should, however, be noted that the opposite trend can be observed in some countries of the region and that there is no private education at all in one of them. In absolute terms, total enrolment in public education rose from 47.8 million in 1970 to 65.3 million in 1976. In private education, the total number of enrolments rose from 8.9 million to 12.8 million over the same period. The greater relative expansion in private education is particularly noticeable in higher education, where the average annual rate of increase was 23.4 per cent over the 1970–76 period. In 1970, three out of every ten students in higher education attended private establishments, while, in 1976/77, the figure was four out of ten.

Enrolments trends by country

Primary education

The figures in Table 1 show overall enrolment trends throughout the region. It is desirable, however, to look at the differences from country to country, which are quite marked in a number of cases and for both sexes. Table 2 shows the enrolment patterns in primary education between 1970 and 1976.

Internal efficiency in primary education

Despite the progress indicated by the figures in Table 2, there are two factors that reduce efficiency in primary education—a low school survival rate and a high number of repeaters.

The survival rate in primary education was recently the subject of a partial study (covering eighteen of the countries in the region) carried out by Unesco. This study showed that, out of every 1,000 children enrolled in the first year of primary education, fewer than 500 reached the fourth year. This is one of the worst problems in the education systems of a large proportion of Latin American countries. It is due to a variety of factors: some of them are inherent in the very structure of the system; others derive from the financial insecurity of broad sectors of the population, which leads families to put their children to work at a very early age. In some cases the problem is due to weaknesses in the educational process—in educational content or teaching methods—which make pupils apathetic and uninterested in a kind of education which they regard as irrelevant or useless.

In a number of Latin American countries, the basic structure of the education system is such that there are in fact, though not ostensibly, two types of primary school, urban and rural. The rural primary school provides a shorter course of study, lasting two, three or four years, in contrast with the five, six or more years in urban primary schools. This difference has an effect on survival-rate statistics. Erroneous figures for survival rates will be obtained if they are calculated on the basis of five or six years' schooling, which is not provided in certain rural areas. In other words, although the pupils in such cases may complete their schooling, their school education is excessively limited in duration. The scale of this problem is clearly illustrated by the fact that, at the beginning of the 1970s, 75 per cent of rural schools were not providing the full course (see Table 3).

TABLE 2. Crude enrolment ratios (national structures)[1] in primary education. Latin America and the Caribbean, by country, 1970 and 1976

Country	1970	1976	Absolute increase
Group 1	%	%	%
Antigua[2]	106.5	114.4[3]	7.9
Argentina	105.7	108.0	2.3
Barbados	102.7	108.2	5.5
Chile	107.2	116.8	9.6
Cuba	119.4	121.9	2.5
Dominica[2]	113.1	107.1	−6.0
Ecuador	97.0	102.2	5.2
Grenada[2]	134.3	107.2	−27.1
Jamaica	100.0	96.8	−3.2
Mexico	104.4	115.9	11.5
Montserrat[2]	112.2	100.0[3]	−12.2
Panama	103.4	125.6	22.2
Peru	113.5	116.0	2.5
St Kitts–Nevis–Anguilla[2]	99.5	110.7[3]	11.2
Saint Lucia[2]	121.1	133.3	12.2
St Vincent[2]	134.4	104.5[3]	−29.9
Group II			
Brazil	81.3	93.0[3]	11.7
Costa Rica	109.6	110.9	1.3
Dominican Republic	101.3	106.0[3]	4.7
Guyana	96.2	99.1	2.9
Suriname	127.4	104.6	−22.8
Trinidad and Tobago	112.2	108.2	−4.0
Uruguay	105.7	91.3	−14.4
Venezuela	94.4	104.0	9.6
Group III			
Bolivia	67.9	80.4	12.5
Colombia	99.8	102.6	2.8
El Salvador	67.5	76.4	8.9
Guatemala	57.7	64.6	6.9
Haiti	48.3	71.3	23.0
Honduras	89.6	89.0	−0.6
Nicaragua	83.0	87.9	4.9
Paraguay	109.3	102.9	−6.4

1. These ratios relate total enrolment in primary education to the population in the 'official' age-group, according to the structures of the national education systems.
2. In the case of this country, the enrolment ratios are given with reservations, in view of the approximate nature of the population data used.
3. Estimated figures.

TABLE 3. Indicators of the internal efficiency of primary-education systems

Country	Normal duration (1)	Cohort starting year (2)	Pupil-years used (3)	Input-output ratio (3)/(1) =(4)	Total number of drop-outs (out of 1,000)	Pupils who completed their studies according to the number of years repeated (out of 1,000)				
						Total	0	1	2	3 and over
			%	%						
Argentina	7	1973	9.56	1.37	339	661	359	206	72	24
Brazil	8	1971	15.07	1.88	696	304	105	104	59	36
Chile	8	1970	12.72	1.59	453	547	238	181	84	44
Colombia	5	1970	9.62	1.92	625	375	188	119	47	21
Costa Rica	6	1970	7.36	1.23	218	782	511	207	52	12
Cuba	6	1970	7.99	1.33	198	802	275	293	156	78
Ecuador	6	1970	8.61	1.43	443	557	284	181	68	24
El Salvador	9	1971	17.34	1.93	729	271	171	75	21	4
Guatemala	6	1970	12.15	2.02	677	323	157	104	43	19
Guyana	6	1970	7.35	1.22	137	863	543	237	65	18
Mexico	6	1974	8.11	1.35	384	616	365	178	55	18
Nicaragua	6	1970	12.53	2.09	734	266	148	82	27	9
Panama	6	1971	7.78	1.30	270	730	353	233	99	45
Paraguay	6	1970	12.16	2.03	599	401	160	134	67	40
Peru	6	1972	8.52	1.42	356	644	302	216	91	35
Suriname	6	1974	11.14	1.86	460	540	131	162	120	127
Uruguay	6	1970	7.70	1.28	105	895	337	296	158	104
Venezuela	6	1970	7.93	1.32	383	616	502	97	15	2

This situation has a number of very bad effects. A very large proportion of the pupils in rural areas cannot go on to secondary education, for which completion of the full primary course is a prerequisite, without moving to an urban area—and not all can do that. Thus the rural population is the victim of a disturbing form of discrimination that favours the urban population. In rural areas, the percentage of people with only three years of primary schooling, together with those who receive no instruction at all, is usually twice and, in some cases, three times the corresponding percentage in urban areas. Not only does such discrimination create, for the individual, a morally inadmissible obstacle to the observance of the universally accepted right to equal educational opportunities, it also deprives society of the potentially valuable contribution of many highly intelligent people whose development is hampered by the difficulties of access to secondary and higher education.

Repeaters
High repetition rates continue to reduce efficiency in primary-school education in the region. In 1970, 15.7 per cent of the pupils enrolled in primary schools (years 1–5) in the region were repeaters. By 1975, this percentage had

dropped slightly, to 13.6 per cent. Bearing in mind that these percentages apply only to the first five years of primary education, we may make the following observations with regard to the region: (a) around 5.9 of the 38.4 million pupils were repeaters in 1970; (b) more than 6 million out of 44.3 million pupils were repeaters in 1975; (c) there was a slight drop in the number of repeaters in the first year of schooling in relation to the total number of pupils in the first five years (I, 44 per cent in 1970 to 42 per cent in 1975; II, 55 per cent in 1970 to 53 per cent in 1975; and III, 51 per cent in 1970 to 50 per cent in 1975); (d) two countries (Brazil and Mexico), which accounted for 59 per cent of the total number of repeaters in the region in 1970, accounted for 65 per cent in 1975.

Another characteristic failure of the education system, which is very widespread in the region, is the high degree of repetition among the same pupils. In 1975, it was estimated that around 14 per cent of the pupils were repeating levels and courses for the second or third time.

The transition from primary to secondary education
The numbers moving from the first to the second level of education have been computed by means of a coefficient found by dividing enrolments in the first year of secondary education (minus any repeaters) by enrolments in the

TABLE 4. Transition ratios (primary to secondary education)

Country	1969/70	1974/75
	%	%
Group I		
Argentina	95	92
Chile	86	78
Cuba	72	97
Panama	—	60
Peru	85	75
Group II		
Brazil	97	99
Colombia	53	—
Costa Rica	64	74
Ecuador	63	57
Guyana	89	84
Venezuela	85	83
Group III		
Bolivia	84	—
El Salvador	68	85
Guatemala	70	—
Trinidad and Tobago	83	—

Note: These transition ratios are obtained by dividing the number of enrolments (minus any repeaters) in the first year of secondary education by the number of enrolments in the last year of primary education—i.e. in the previous year. It should be borne in mind that the number of years of study at each educational level differs from country to country.

preceding year, which is the last year of primary education. This method is based on the assumption that most of the new secondary students were in the last year of primary school in the previous year.

Although information is incomplete in some cases, a broad picture of the situation may be obtained from the coefficients in Table 4, which gives data relating to fifteen countries for the years 1969/70 and 1974/75. The overall transition level in 1974/75 ranges from around 60 per cent in Panama and Ecuador to around 100 per cent in Brazil and Cuba. Only in the case of ten countries are the figures for both periods comparable. Six of these countries (Chile, Argentina, Peru, Ecuador, Guyana and Venezuela) show a downward trend, but there was an increase in transition ratios in four other countries (Cuba, Costa Rica, Brazil and El Salvador).

Enrolment trends in secondary education
Between 1960 and 1977, secondary-school enrolments in the region rose from 2.8 million to 14.1 million, a relative increase of 397 per cent. This is obviously a great improvement, but it would have been even greater were it not for the failure of some rural primary schools to provide instruction for the number of years required for admission to secondary education, as has already been mentioned. Secondary-school enrolments in 1976 were distributed as follows: the number of pupils receiving a general education, which prepares students for higher education, represented 70.5 per cent of the total number of enrolments. In trade, technical and vocational education as a whole, the commercial branch accounted for over 50 per cent of enrolments and industrial education for over 26 per cent (see Table 5).

It is difficult to compare the different countries with regard to the increase in enrolments during the years under review and the distribution of enrolments among the different branches and types of education at this level because different criteria are used for determining the length of the various courses or because the criteria themselves vary. For example, during this period Costa Rica, Chile and Peru decided that primary-school teachers should be trained at the higher-education level. Since 1970, Ecuador has made the first phase of teacher-training and other types of education part of a general education. It is extremely difficult to determine how far the distribution of pupils among the different vocational branches of secondary education meets employment needs, because of the complexity of the problem itself and the lack of studies on employment prospects. However, the high percentage of pupils in general secondary education would seem to be disproportionate to the number taking vocational courses, and possibly bears no relation to economic and social requirements.

Expansion of higher education: distribution by specialized studies
During the period under review, the transition ratio between secondary and higher education showed a marked increase over earlier periods, rising from 24.66 per cent in 1966 to 34 per cent in 1975. In absolute terms, the scale of the increase in higher-education enrolments over such a relatively short period of

TABLE 5. Secondary education: trade, technical and vocational education. Pupils by field of study and by sex, in the most recent year available

Country and year	Sex	Total number of pupils	Fields of study according to ISCED[1]					
			Commercial programmes	Trade, craft and industrial programmes	Technology	Agricultural, forestry and fishery programmes	Other programmes[2]	Not specified
			%	%	%	%	%	%
Antigua	MF	102	26.5	—	53.9	—	19.6	—
1975								
Argentina	MF	846 200	51.5	41.6	—	2.3	4.1	0.5
1977	F	403 039	66.2	26.0	—	1.1	6.2	0.5
Brazil	MF	782 827	60.8	20.9	—	3.0	14.8	0.5
1974	F	338 538	69.4	10.6	—	0.8	18.6	0.6
Chile	MF	168 823	32.8	45.1	—	1.9	20.2	—
1977	F	77 269	51.5	4.2	—	1.0	43.3	—
Colombia	MF	308 823	45.2	16.7	—	6.5	2.8	28.7
1977								
Cuba	MF	145 205	17.8	—	56.8	25.4	—	—
1976	F	42 594	40.9	—	41.5	17.6	—	—
Dominica	MF	567	35.1	4.2	5.3	2.6	52.8	—
1976	F	464	42.9	—	—	—	57.1	—
Ecuador[3]	MF	42 940	75.6	12.9	—	7.1	4.2	0.1
1976	F	25 857	93.5	0.1	—	1.1	5.1	0.1
El Salvador	MF	25 762	82.1	10.4	—	5.3	2.2	—
1976	F	11 500	93.9	2.1	—	0.6	3.4	—
Montserrat	MF	57	100.0	—	—	—	—	—
1975	F	24	100.0	—	—	—	—	—
Panama	MF	43 505	49.6	19.6	—	3.3	5.9	21.6
1977	F	22 961	68.9	0.8	—	0.9	9.9	19.5
Paraguay	MF	5 427	77.2	5.9	—	8.1	8.8	—
1977	F	2 363	84.5	1.0	—	—	14.5	—
Saint Lucia	MF	230	26.1	49.6	24.3	—	—	—
1975	F	59	93.2	6.8	—	—	—	—
St Vincent	MF	108	28.7	14.8	35.2	—	21.3	—
1975	F	31	100.0	—	—	—	—	—
Suriname[3]	MF	4 472	—	24.0	52.7	12.9	10.4	—
1977	F	1 145	—	55.6	1.0	3.7	39.7	—
Venezuela[3]	MF	158 582	4.1	8.8	—	2.3	5.6	79.2
1976	F	79 483	7.0	2.0	—	0.8	8.7	81.5

1. International Standard Classification of Education
2. These programmes include fine and applied arts, religion and theology, health-related auxiliary programmes, home economics (domestic science), transport and communications and service trades.
3. Full-time courses only.

time is quite striking. Between 1960 and 1977, the number of students at this level of education rose from little over 500,000 to 4,267,000, a relative increase of 682 per cent. But it should be noted that higher education accounts for only 5.4 per cent of the average enrolment in the Latin American and Caribbean education system as a whole.

TABLE 6. Regional distribution of enrolments in higher education by field of study in 1970 and 1975 (percentages)

Field of study	1970	1975
Scientific and technological disciplines	38.2	38.6
Natural sciences	5.5	5.2
Engineering	15.5	15.9
Medicine	13.6	13.7
Agronomy	3.6	3.8
Other fields	59.4	50.2
Humanities	11.5	8.2
Education	11.1	9.6
Fine arts	4.7	2.9
Law	11.4	8.4
Social sciences	20.7	21.1
Not specified	2.4	11.2
TOTAL	100.0	100.0

Table 6 shows the distribution of higher-education enrolments by field of study in percentages. It covers the years 1970 and 1975, the latter being the last year for which the region as a whole can be assessed from the available data. It will be seen that there is a decline in the proportion of enrolments in the humanities, education, fine arts and law and a very slight increase in the social sciences. The percentage of students enrolled in scientific and technological disciplines has varied little in the period under review. It should be noted that the percentages of students enrolled in the natural sciences and in agronomy remained relatively low in 1975. On the other hand, there was a high percentage of enrolments in the 'not specified' category in 1975. These were students, enrolled in the common basic phase of higher education, who were not specifically considered by field of study.

Table 7 gives a country-by-country analysis of both the fields of study and the programme levels of students in higher education. Owing to the shortage of data in this area, Table 7 refers only to the most recent year for which statistics are available since 1974. Similarly, because it is difficult to compare available data, the humanities, education, fine arts, law and the social sciences have been placed in a single column (other fields).

The types of programme correspond to the programmes given in the International Standard Classification of Education (ISCED). They are defined as follows:

A. ISCED category level 5: education at the third level, of the type that leads to an award not equivalent to a first university degree.

B. ISCED category level 6: education at the third level, first stage, of the type that leads to a first university degree or equivalent.

C. ISCED category level 7: education at the third level, second stage, of the type that leads to a post-graduate university degree or equivalent.

Enrolment distribution for both field of study and type of programme is known in the case of only sixteen of the twenty-one countries shown in Table 7. In only five of these countries are the three types of programmes (A, B and C) available. The other countries state that they provide A and B type programmes (five countries) and B and C type programmes (two countries). Lastly, four countries state that they provide only B-type programmes. None the less, in the seven countries where C type programmes (leading to a post-graduate university degree or equivalent) are available, enrolment figures are relatively low. In the vast majority of these countries, a very high proportion of the students in higher education (between 85 and 100 per cent) are enrolled in B type programmes.

The distribution of students by field of study can be analysed in only seventeen countries, owing to the high proportion of students in the 'not specified' category in Brazil, Costa Rica, the Dominican Republic and Venezuela. In five of the seventeen countries (Cuba, El Salvador, Haiti, Mexico, and Trinidad and Tobago), more than half of the students were taking scientific or technological courses. In Haiti, around 40 per cent of the total number of students were studying medicine, and 30 per cent in Uruguay. In eight other countries, this figure varies between 16 and 23 per cent. Engineering is the other branch of study in the scientific and technological field that attracts a higher proportion of enrolments, particularly in Chile (29 per cent), Mexico (28 per cent), Peru (24 per cent), Cuba and Honduras (22 per cent), and El Salvador and Trinidad and Tobago (21 per cent).

In general, the natural sciences and agriculture account for no more than 9 per cent of the total number of students, except in Cuba (11 per cent), Trinidad and Tobago (13 per cent) and Uruguay (10 per cent) for agriculture, and Jamaica (27 per cent), Barbados (25 per cent) and Trinidad and Tobago (17 per cent) for the natural sciences.

The fields of study classified as 'other fields' (humanities, education, fine arts, law and the social sciences) generally account for a high proportion of total enrolments, although again there are considerable differences among the countries listed in Table 7. The proportion is under 50 per cent in only four countries (Cuba, 48 per cent; Mexico, 39 per cent; El Salvador, 47 per cent; Haiti, 21 per cent). These fields of study account for the highest number of enrolments in the other thirteen countries (excluding the four already mentioned, where the 'not specified' percentage is significant).

The relative distribution by field of study naturally tends to vary

TABLE 7. Higher education: students by field of study and type of programmes, in the most recent year available (both sexes)

Country and year	Type of pro-gramme[1]	Number of students	Natural sciences	Engineer-ing	Medicine	Agronomy	Other fields[2]	Not specified
			%	%	%	%	%	%
Argentina 1976	Total	601 395	4.2	13.9	16.4	5.9	58.4	1.2
Barbados[3] 1976	Total	1 140	25.1	—	—	—	74.9	—
	A	39	—	—	—	—	100.0	—
	B	1 054	26.5	—	—	—	73.5	—
	C	47	10.6	—	—	—	89.4	—
Bolivia 1976	Total	51 585	2.1	13.5	16.1	2.5	65.8	—
Brazil 1975	Total	1 089 808	8.2	8.2	7.6	1.7	48.3	26.0[4]
Chile 1977	Total	131 793	—	—	—	—	—	—
	B	130 676	3.4	29.1	12.0	5.0	50.5	—
	C	1 117	—	—	—	—	—	—
Colombia 1977	Total	237 477	2.6	15.4	9.8	4.2	68.0	—
	B	232 765	2.7	15.4	9.7	4.2	68.0	—
	C	4 712	5.6	11.2	17.1	1.5	64.6	—
Costa Rica 1977	Total	38 629	5.7	9.5	8.3	5.9	38.0	32.6
Cuba 1974	Total	68 051	5.8	22.1	10.7	10.9	48.4	2.1
	B	68 051						
Dominican Republic[5] 1975	Total	28 628	2.2	13.6	20.7	2.2	30.5	30.8[4]
	A	3 819	12.7	—	16.2	—	71.1	—
	B	24 809	0.6	15.7	21.4	2.6	24.2	35.5
El Salvador 1975	Total	28 281	2.8	20.8[6]	22.6	6.8	47.0[6]	—
	A	1 372	—	34.0	23.9	19.4	22.7	—
	B	26 909	2.9	20.1	22.5	6.2	48.3	—
Guatemala[7] 1977	Total	29 234	1.9	16.5	21.5	8.6	51.5	—
	B	29 234						
Haiti 1976	Total	3 309	2.2	17.2	39.5	5.8	21.3	14.0
	A	836	—	—	32.3	—	12.4	55.3
	B	2 473	3.0	23.0	41.9	7.8	24.3	—
Honduras 1976	Total	15 499	4.8	21.6	16.9	2.1	54.1	0.5
	A	2 475	25.6	5.0	—	13.3	52.9	3.2
	B	13 024	0.8	24.7	20.1	—	54.4	—

TABLE 7 (*continued*)

Country and year	Type of programme[1]	Number of students	Field of study — Scientific and technological disciplines				Other fields[2]	Not specified
			Natural sciences	Engineering	Medicine	Agronomy		
			%	%	%	%	%	%
Jamaica[3] 1976	Total	4 091	26.8	0.6	17.7	—	54.9	—
	A	631	—	4.0	13.8	—	82.2	—
	B	3 078	33.5	—	18.0	—	48.5	—
	C	382	17.5	—	21.2	—	61.3	—
Mexico 1976	Total	539 372	5.7	27.6	21.9	5.0	38.6	1.2
Panama 1976	Total	30 473	5.6	13.6	10.0	3.2	57.6	10.0
	A	4 592	0.2	33.9	0.5	1.5	26.8	37.1
	B	25 856	6.4	10.0	11.7	3.5	63.2	5.2
	C	25	100.0	—	—	—	—	—
Peru 1977	Total	233 420	2.1	24.5	8.9	4.4	57.0	3.1
	A	33 420	0.6	24.3	6.2	3.0	62.6	3.3
	B	198 979	2.4	24.6	9.4	4.7	56.3	2.6
	C	1 021	—	—	—	—	—	100.0
Suriname 1977	Total	900	4.7	—	21.4	—	73.9	—
	B	900						
Trinidad and Tobago 1977	Total	2 477	16.8	21.1	—	13.4	48.7	—
	A	68	2.9	—	—	—	97.1	—
	B	2 019	19.1	24.1	—	12.7	44.1	—
	C	390	7.4	9.5	—	19.2	63.9	—
Uruguay 1975	Total	32 627	1.3	6.3	30.2	10.4	51.4	0.4
	A	389	—	—	100.0	—	—	—
	B	32 238	1.3	6.4	29.5	10.5	51.9	0.4
Venezuela[8] 1976	Total	247 518	6.7	17.1	8.4	3.9	36.9	27.0
	B	247 518						

1. Type of programme according to the International Standard Classification of Education (ISCED):
   A = programmes leading to an award not equivalent to a university degree (ISCED, category level 5);
   B = programmes leading to a first university degree or equivalent (ISCED, category level 6);
   C = programmes leading to a post-graduate university degree or equivalent (ISCED, category level 7).
2. Includes humanities, education, fine arts, law and social sciences.
3. The University of the West Indies only.
4. Mostly students enrolled in the first year or in the preparatory year (general studies).
5. The Universidad Autónoma de Santo Domingo only.
6. Architecture is classified under 'Engineering'.
7. The Universidad de San Carlos only.
8. Universities or equivalent establishments and non-university teacher-training.

TABLE 8. Higher education: graduates by field of study and type of programme, in the most recent year available (both sexes)

Country and year	Type of pro- gramme[1]	Number of graduates	Field of study					
			Scientific and technological disciplines					
			Natural sciences	Engineer- ing	Medicine	Agronomy	Other fields[2]	Not specified
			%	%	%	%	%	%
Bolivia[3]	Total	1 973	1.2	12.5	32.3	7.1	46.9	—
1976	A	234	—	20.5	0.9	—	78.6	—
	B	1 739	1.4	11.4	36.6	8.1	42.5	—
Brazil	Total	153 065	9.4	8.2	9.8	2.0	70.6	—
1974	B	150 226	9.3	7.8	9.7	1.9	71.3	—
	C	2 839	14.6	27.6	13.7	8.3	35.8	—
Chile	Total	14 474	2.4	17.8	14.3	4.8	60.7	—
1977	A	383	11.5	1.3	5.0	5.5	76.7	—
	B	13 824	1.5	18.5	14.7	4.8	60.5	—
	C	267	34.8	3.7	7.1	3.8	50.6	—
Colombia	Total	18 780	3.5	13.5	10.8	4.4	67.8	—
1977	B	18 780						
Costa Rica	Total	2 307	3.4	7.2	17.9	4.9	66.6	—
1976	A	501	—	5.2	21.0	—	73.8	—
	B	1 033	5.1	6.7	4.5	—	83.7	—
	C	773	3.2	9.1	33.8	14.6	39.3	—
Cuba	Total	6 106	8.0	14.7	27.1	13.0	37.2	—
1974	B	6 106						
Dominican	Total	1 173	6.6	14.5	37.3	3.0	38.6	—
Republic[4]	A	412	7.5	—	24.5	—	68.0	—
1975	B	761	6.2	22.3	44.2	4.6	22.7	—
El Salvador	Total	1 102	3.4	30.5	16.8	11.3	38.0	—
1975	A	655	—	35.9	24.6	8.2	31.3	—
	B	447	8.5	22.6	5.4	15.7	47.8	—
Guatemala[5]	Total	1 443	1.5	10.7	25.8	5.7	56.3	—
1977	B	1 443						
Haiti	Total	265	8.3	—	69.8	10.9	11.0	—
1976								
Honduras	Total	—	—	—	—	—	—	—
1976	A	—	—	—	—	—	—	—
	B	385	0.8	23.9	27.8	—	47.5	—
Jamaica[6]	Total	1 281	22.0	8.8	8.2	2.6	58.4	—
1977								

TABLE 8 (*continued*)

Country and year	Type of programme[1]	Number of graduates	Natural sciences	Engineering	Medicine	Agronomy	Other fields[2]	Not specified
			%	%	%	%	%	%
Panama	Total	1 668	26.6	8.5	17.4	1.0	40.9	5.6
1976	A	315	39.4	21.9	5.1	—	33.3	0.3
	B	1 350	23.4	5.3	20.3	1.2	43.0	6.8
	C	3	100.0	—	—	—	—	—
Peru[7]	Total	5 450	—	24.7	8.6	3.0	63.7	—
1977	A	3 015	—	42.3	15.5	5.4	36.8	—
	B	2 435	—	3.0	—	—	97.0	—
Trinidad and Tobago[6]	Total	585	12.6	21.1	—	11.8	54.4	—
1977	A	6	—	—	—	—	100.0	—
	B	458	15.1	24.3	—	12.9	47.7	—
	C	121	4.1	10.7	—	8.3	76.9	—
Uruguay	Total	2 049	2.3	2.8	30.8	12.8	39.8	11.5
1975	A	337	6.8	—	3.0	—	90.2	—
	B	1 690	1.4	3.4	35.4	15.5	30.4	13.9
	C	22	—	—	100.0	—	—	—
Venezuela	Total	12 940	6.9	19.4	12.1	4.8	54.1	2.7
1976	B	12 940						

The header above spans: **Field of study** over all field columns, with **Scientific and technological disciplines** spanning Natural sciences, Engineering, Medicine, Agronomy.

1. See Note 1, Table 7.
2. Includes humanities, education, fine arts, law and the social sciences.
3. Does not include teacher training at the third level of education, in non-university establishments.
4. Only the Universidad autónoma de Santo Domingo.
5. Only the Universidad de San Carlos.
6. Only the University of the West Indies.
7. The data refer only to university graduates.

according to the type of programme (A, B or C), as may be seen in Table 7 (for example, in the cases of Colombia and Peru). None the less, as the available data are extremely limited and a very high proportion of enrolments are in B type programmes, it is not easy to draw general conclusions about this aspect of enrolment distribution.

Graduates
The analysis of graduate trends presents certain problems because information is not available for all the countries in the region; furthermore, the number of

graduates varies considerably from one year to the next. The main reason for this is that the term 'graduate' has different meanings in the various Latin American and Caribbean countries. The number of graduates differs considerably depending on whether one means university leavers or degree-holders. If the latter category is considered, the number of graduates tends to be low since, in order to obtain a degree, university leavers have to continue their studies and either submit a thesis or take a degree examination. In general, most university leavers fail to complete this final stage of their studies. This point needs to be borne in mind in studying trends in the number of graduates in Latin America and the Caribbean.

Table 8 gives the available data on graduates, classified by field of study and by type of programme. The explanations given in connection with Table 7 referring to students also apply to Table 8. Data on graduates are even scarcer than data on student enrolment. Table 8 refers to only seventeen of the thirty-two countries and territories discussed in this report (although it should be borne in mind that seven of them have no institutions of higher education).

It will be seen that, in general, the distribution of graduates follows the pattern discernible in student enrolments. Comparing it with Table 7, however, we see that Table 8 shows that the number of graduates in scientific and technological disciplines accounted for over 50 per cent of the total number of graduates in eight countries (Bolivia, Cuba, El Salvador, Haiti, Honduras, Panama, the Dominican Republic and Uruguay). In Cuba, El Salvador and Haiti, the figures simply reflect the fact that most students were enrolled in this field of study, although in a smaller proportion. In the case of the other countries, it might be inferred that the level of efficiency of education is higher for science-and-technology students than for students in other fields of study. This could be explained in some degree by the higher drop-out rates in the non-scientific fields of study. In a number of countries, however, the percentage of non-science graduates is higher than the percentage of science enrolments, for example in Brazil, Peru and Trinidad and Tobago.

Teachers

Quantitative trends

The number of teachers rose much more quickly than the number of students, increasing from a total of 1,156,000 in 1960 to 2,274,000 in 1970 (practically doubling) and to 3,547,000 in 1977, which is more than one and a half times the 1970 figure. Table 9 breaks down these figures by level of education. They call for a number of observations:

In primary education, the number of teachers rose by around 300,000 every five years up to 1970. Between 1970 and 1977, it increased by more than 800,000. While primary teachers represented 66 per cent of the total number of teachers in 1960, they accounted for 61 per cent in 1977.

In secondary education, the number of teachers rose by about 200,000 to

TABLE 9. Teachers by level of education in the region. Both sexes, 1960–77 (in thousands)

Level of education	1960	1965	1970	1977	1977 index	
					1960 = 100	1970 = 100
First	764	1 052	1 339	2 154	282	161
Second	326	497	779	1 005	308	129
Third	66	108	156	388	588	249
TOTAL	1 156	1 657	2 274	3 547	307	156

250,000 every five years. The proportion of secondary teachers in relation to the total number of teachers was the same in 1960 as in 1977 (28 per cent).

In higher education, the number of teachers rose by 40,000 to 50,000 every five years up to 1970. Between 1970 and 1977, there was an increase of more than 230,000 teachers. In relation to the total number of teachers, the proportion of teachers in higher education rose from 6 per cent in 1960 to 11 per cent in 1977.

Table 10 shows teacher/pupil ratios. It will be noted that in primary education the teacher/pupil ratio fell by two points between 1960 and 1965 and by 4 points between 1970 and 1977. In fact, this ratio increased in eight

TABLE 10. Average teacher/pupil ratio in the region (1960–77)

Level of education	1960	1965	1970	1977
First	34	32	32	28
Second	12	13	13	14
Third	8	8	10	11

countries, remained unchanged in five countries and dropped in the other countries. Table 11 gives the teacher/pupil ratio in primary education by country for the period from 1960 to the most recent year for which data are available (generally 1976 or 1977). Table 11 shows that, while the average number of pupils per teacher varies considerably between countries, it has also fluctuated a good deal from one period to another. None the less, the trend is definitely downward, that is to say, the average number of pupils per teacher is lower, as may be seen from Table 11. It is to be noted, in particular, that the number of countries with a higher teacher/pupil ratio (1:41 and over) fell from six in 1960 to three in 1977, while in 1960 there was only one country with a ratio of 1:25 or under, compared with eight countries in this category in 1977.

TABLE 11. Break-down of the thirty-two countries according to the teacher/pupil ratio in primary education

Number of pupils per teacher	Number of countries		
	1960	1970	1977
25 or less	1	3	8
26–30	8	9	6
31–35	8	6	7
36–40	9	9	8
41 and over	6	5	3
TOTAL	32	32	32

In secondary education, the regional teacher/pupil ratio increased by one point between 1960 and 1965 and by a further point between 1970 and 1977. Despite this increase, it should be noted that the teacher/pupil ratio in secondary education is comparatively low in a number of countries, particularly in countries where there has been an increase. In 1960, sixteen countries (out of thirty-two) could claim teacher/pupil ratios of 1:15 or less. The number of such countries had fallen to twelve by 1970 and to eight by 1977. In only four out of the thirty-two countries was the teacher/pupil ratio in secondary education 1:26 or over in the period 1960–77.

Lastly, the teacher/student ratio in higher education rose from 1:8 to 1:10 between 1965 and 1970, and from 1:10 to 1:11 between 1970 and 1977. It is interesting to note that teacher/student ratios in the region were relatively low in 1977 (1:28 in primary education, 1:14 in secondary education and 1:11 in higher education). The average teacher/pupil ratios in developing countries were 1:34 in primary education, 1:21 in secondary education, and 1:15 in higher education. The ratios in developed countries were 1:21 in primary education, 1:16 in secondary education, and 1:14 in higher education.

The average level of education of the population

In overall terms, the average level of education in the region as a whole has risen appreciably over the last two decades. According to data for 1950, relating to Latin America and the Caribbean, with the exception of those countries that were not independent at the time, some 49 per cent of the population aged 15 and over had not attended school or had left school before completing the first year of schooling; some 44 per cent had attended school for a time without completing their primary education, and only 7 per cent had received a complete primary education; only around 6 per cent had received a secondary or technical education; only some 2 per cent had completed this course of study; and no more than about 1 per cent entered university. Details of attainments in the different stages of education are given in Table 12.

TABLE 12. Proportion of the population who have had some education

Country	Year	Age-group	Level of education reached (percentage of the population)		
			Less than secondary education[1]	Secondary education[2]	More than secondary education
Antigua	1960	25+	92.0	7.4	0.6
Argentina	1970	25+	80.7	15.3	4.0
Barbados	1970	25+	34.8	64.0	1.2
Brazil	1970	25+	88.7	9.3	2.0
Chile	1970	25+	69.6	26.6	3.8
Colombia	1973	20+	78.3	18.4	3.3
Costa Rica	1973	25+	83.0	11.2	5.8
Dominica	1960	15+	93.1	6.4	0.5
Dominican Republic	1970	25+	86.0	12.1	1.9
Ecuador	1974	25+	85.6	11.2	3.2
El Salvador	1971	25+	93.0	6.1	0.9
Grenada	1960	15+	91.8	7.7	0.5
Guatemala	1973	25+	93.9	4.9	1.2
Guyana	1960	15+	89.0	10.6	0.4
Haiti	1971	25+	96.0	3.7	0.3
Honduras	1974	25+	93.6	5.4	1.0
Jamaica	1960	25+	94.1	5.4	0.5
Mexico	1970	20+	89.8	7.6	2.6
Panama	1970	25+	78.4	17.4	4.2
Paraguay	1972	25+	87.6	10.4	2.0
Peru	1972	25+	82.1	13.4	4.5
Trinidad and Tobago	1970	25+	86.2	12.6	1.2
Uruguay	1975	25+	76.2	17.5	6.3
Venezuela	1961	25+	93.2	5.3	1.5

1. Includes: 'no school education', 'incomplete primary education', and 'complete primary education'.
2. Includes: 'incomplete secondary education' and 'complete secondary education'.

Education reforms

The expansion of education and the new educational problems brought about by society's growing expectations and demands in relation to education have led to an education-reform movement in the region. In some cases, the reforms have been thorough and comprehensive; in others, they have been confined to certain sectors or levels of education.

In the section above, dealing with the recommendations and guidelines of the conferences of ministers, reference has been made to certain trends which have influenced these reforms. To put the matter briefly, the nature and basic objectives of this movement are rooted in a concern to democratize education and to improve its quality. The movement also seeks to relate education more closely to economic and social development and to strengthen the identity and distinctive features of each country through the region's education systems. This has been achieved to a greater degree in those newly independent countries where forms of education transplanted from their former mother countries had previously prevailed.

The growing importance attached to pre-school education and the consequent expansion of this level of education have been increasingly reflected in structural reforms. Yet pre-school education, which is so vital to the intellectual development of children, and is such an effective way of making up for inadequacies and shortcomings in their upbringing which originate in their socio-cultural background, is not generally available to those who are most in need of it; it is rarely provided in rural areas. It is expanding principally in the private sector, and is beyond the reach of those who have not sufficient financial means to meet the expenditure involved.

In some countries, the duration of compulsory education has been extended. In a number of cases, primary education and the initial years of secondary education have been combined to produce a more effective basic education course.

In most of the countries, secondary education is divided into two phases: a common first phase and a diversified second phase. In recent reforms, the tendency has been to provide more specialized studies with various subject options or more vocational education courses that prepare pupils for specific occupations.

In higher education, there has been a tendency towards structural integration. In particular, departments have been established instead of the traditional faculties and schools. Another trend, which in a sense runs counter to this, is the establishment of specialized institutions to provide training for specific professions (university colleges of agriculture, education or engineering, or higher polytechnical institutes). More short courses are being introduced, and post-graduate courses are frequently organized within the framework of lifelong education.

More attention is now being paid to the various forms of adult education such as literacy training, supplementary education for people who missed part of their school education, accelerated vocational training and job training within the framework of economic development plans.

Many curricular reforms have been introduced in the region. Some countries have established curriculum-development departments or divisions which are responsible for curricular reform and for improving the quality of educational content. Costa Rica, El Salvador, Guatemala, Guyana, Honduras, Jamaica, Panama, Saint Lucia, Suriname, Trinidad and Tobago, and Venezuela are among the countries that have taken such steps. In the Caribbean subregion, the University of the West Indies has been playing an important part in curriculum renewal, teacher-education and the production of teaching materials.

New material is being included in curricula on questions of contemporary interest or which have never been given adequate attention, despite their importance, such as environmental education, population education, sex and family education, and education in health and nutrition. But attempts to bring about renewal have, perhaps, been most evident in the reform of syllabuses for the sciences and their technological applications. Brazil, Mexico, Peru, Venezuela and most of the Caribbean countries have made the greatest effort in this direction. The movement in favour of the integrated teaching of the sciences has gained ground. Special importance is now attached to the provision of the necessary equipment and materials. Teaching materials present a twofold problem, for in some cases they are in short supply and in others they are not used to full capacity. To remedy the shortage, equipment has been imported at considerable expense, very often by using foreign credit. In some cases, it has proved difficult to adapt such equipment to the local situation and to find staff able to use and maintain it. A great deal of attention is being given to low-cost equipment built in small workshops in the schools themselves, with the help of teachers and pupils, or mass-produced from local raw materials. In some countries considerable progress has been made in improving the content of textbooks and their effectiveness as teaching aids, particularly those used in primary and secondary education.

It is undeniable that, in terms of quality, the effectiveness of education systems is primarily determined by their teacher-education systems.

Therefore, one of the most significant indicators of the quality of education is the level of initial and in-service teacher-training. Many of the teachers in the region do not hold specific teaching qualifications, a long-standing problem that has yet to be solved. However, according to recent estimates by Unesco's Regional Office for Education in Latin America and the Caribbean, the percentage of unqualified teachers is declining, as may be seen from Table 13.

There is a trend towards demanding higher qualifications in teacher-education, and this is reflected in an increase in the length of courses. In some

TABLE 13. Latin America and the Caribbean. Trends in the percentage of unqualified teachers in primary or basic education in some countries in the region

Percentage	1960	1965	1970	1975
Less than 30	Argentina	Argentina	Argentina	Argentina
	Cuba	Chile	Chile	Chile
	El Salvador	Costa Rica	Costa Rica	Costa Rica
	Panama	Guatemala	Cuba	Cuba
	Trinidad and Tobago	Panama	Ecuador	Ecuador
	Uruguay	Trinidad and Tobago	El Salvador	El Salvador
		Uruguay	Guatemala	Guatemala
		Venezuela	Mexico	Honduras
			Panama	Mexico
			Paraguay	Nicaragua
			Trinidad and Tobago	Panama
			Uruguay	Paraguay
			Venezuela	Peru
				Trinidad and Tobago
				Uruguay
				Venezuela
30 to 50	Brazil	Brazil	Bolivia	Bolivia
	Chile	Cuba	Brazil	Brazil
	Guatemala	El Salvador	Colombia	Colombia
	Paraguay	Mexico	Honduras	
	Peru	Paraguay	Nicaragua	
			Peru	
Over 50	Bolivia	Bolivia	Dominican Republic	Dominican Republic
	Colombia	Colombia	Haiti	Haiti
	Costa Rica	Dominican Republic		
	Dominican Republic	Ecuador		
	Ecuador	Haiti		
	Haiti	Honduras		
	Honduras	Nicaragua		
	Mexico	Peru		
	Nicaragua			
	Venezuela			

countries, primary teachers are now trained at the higher-education level, instead of at secondary level. This is the case in Argentina, Barbados, Bolivia, Brazil, Chile, Costa Rica, El Salvador, Paraguay, Peru, Trinidad and Tobago and Uruguay. Of course, most secondary-school teachers are trained in institutions of higher education. In many countries, efforts have been stepped up to provide initial and further training for unqualified teachers and refresher courses for qualified teachers in the subjects they teach and methods of teaching them.

Advances have been made in a number of countries in regard to the professional, administrative and financial status of teachers, particularly with a view to giving teachers a degree of security and providing a sound basis for a teaching career, through suitable legislation. Argentina, Bolivia, Brazil, Chile, Colombia, Costa Rica, El Salvador, Guatemala, Honduras, Mexico, Peru, Uruguay and Venezuela have carried through important reforms in this direction over the past few years.

Spectacular progress has been made in recent years in the use of the mass media for educational purposes, which are particularly suited to this region in view of its geographical nature, the vast distances, the scattered population, the lack of buildings and amenities, and other circumstances.

Some form of educational television service is provided in most of the countries. Many countries in the region are extending this line of activity. Several categories of programmes involving the use of radio and television for educational purposes may be singled out: (a) those intended to compensate for the lack of schools among certain sectors of the population, particularly in rural areas, as in the case of the radio schools; (b) systems usually intended for adults of all ages, based on the 'open university' principle, covering a wide range of programmes providing teacher-training, supplementary education, vocational training, higher education, etc.; and (c) programmes designed to assist the teacher's work in the classroom. A wide variety of methods is used for the purpose: 'teleclasses' (Mexico), radio guidance for students to whom printed material has been circulated (the Santa Maria radio schools in the Dominican Republic), correspondence courses (Programa de Educación de Adultos por Correspondencia (PEAC) in Guatemala); a combination of television with semi-programmed texts and group dynamics (Preparatoria Abierta, Monterrey, Mexico); educational televised fiction (João da Silva, Fundação Centro Brasileiro de Televisão Educativa (FCBTE) Brazil); a combination of television and programmed instruction (Centro de Investigación y Desarrollo de la Educación (CIDE) National Television Service, Chile); the presentation of a 'puzzle' or 'competition' on the television screen, to be solved collectively by small study groups (educational television in the state of Maranhão, Brazil); education in vernacular languages for country-dwellers with their participation in broadcasts (radio schools in Bolivia, Guatemala and other countries); a combination of programmed material with television and the use of computers (the SACI Project for Advanced Satellite Interdisciplinary Communications, Natal, state of Rio Grande do Norte, Brazil).

The movement towards the development of educational research in the region is fairly recent, and not a few of the education reforms now being undertaken lack the experimental and scientific support that this kind of research can provide. None the less, interest in research would seem to be growing, to judge by the increasing number of education-research establishments and the education-research work carried out by many universities and by private foundations and groups. Experiments, especially in teaching methods, are being carried out in secondary schools and other secondary-education establishments. Besides this, important research studies have been conducted on general aspects of the operation and efficiency of education systems and on the relations between these systems and economic and social development. These studies have dealt with such subjects as educational opportunities, education and employment, and the financing and costs of education. Deserving of special mention in this connection is the extensive work being carried out within the framework of the project on Development and Education in Latin America and the Caribbean, sponsored jointly by Unesco, the United Nations Economic Commission for Latin America and the United Nations Development Programme (UNDP). The main aim of this project is to analyse the complex relations between development and education, which have recently undergone a number of qualitative changes as a result of the large-scale expansion of education and the new situations created by the dynamics of development in Latin America. Some of the project studies are carried out with the direct co-operation of governments and academic institutions of countries in the region, so that their recommendations are directed towards the solution of the specific, and by no means identical, problems of the different societies in the region. Certain priority aspects or major research and policy areas have been selected from the vast range of issues: (a) the role of education in rural society; (b) the relations between employment and education; (c) the role of the university in economic and social development; (d) the capacity of education systems to meet demands for change and to promote social change; and (e) the pattern of the relations between development and education in the different styles of development that are characteristic of the various countries of the region, the analysis of which may suggest ways of solving the problems confronting other countries in similar situations.

The education situation and trends in the Caribbean subregion

In the main working document prepared by the Unesco Secretariat for the Mexico City Conference there is a separate section dealing with certain specific features of education in the English-speaking countries of the Caribbean and its achievements. This seems to be justified for two fundamental reasons. First, certain educational institutions and models bear the distinctive stamp of the colonial past of these countries; second, although some of the Caribbean countries had taken part in previous conferences of ministers of the region, far more of them attended the Mexico City Conference. It was therefore decided, during the course of the preliminary studies on the education situation, to consider this group of countries separately as a mark of the achievement represented by the unprecedented participation of so many of them, including a number of newly independent countries. The working document prepared by the Unesco Secretariat refers to the education situation and trends in the Caribbean as follows:

In pre-primary education, many Member States in this subregion have attained high enrolment rates in comparison with other countries of the region. Among them, special mention should be made of the case of Barbados and Suriname which, towards the end of the current decade, have succeeded, respectively, in enrolling in pre-primary education 60 per cent and 85 per cent of five-year-old children. Grenada, Guyana, Jamaica and Saint Lucia are also making considerable efforts in this direction. The Governments of Jamaica and Suriname have given active support to the development of pre-primary education by taking over responsibility for the training of teachers and by awarding grants to encourage its expansion.

One of the outstanding features in the majority of countries of the subregion is the high rate of school enrolment in the 7–12 age bracket. The main thrust in these countries is now directed towards qualitative improvement. Considerable efforts are being made to introduce changes in content and experiments in primary education are at present going on in such countries as Barbados, Jamaica, Guyana, Saint Lucia, Suriname, and Trinidad and Tobago, where curriculum reform has been combined with efforts to develop new teaching materials. To some extent, at both primary and secondary levels, various Caribbean Member States have also made efforts to promote endogenous development by attempting to replace textbooks and materials from outside the subregion by the works of local authors and consultants. This applies particularly to Barbados, Jamaica, Saint Lucia, and Trinidad and Tobago. Since gaining its independence in 1975, Suriname has been endeavouring to adapt curriculum content to its development needs and strategies. In the same way, countries have realized that their Ministries of Education need to be suitably equipped for curriculum planning and evaluation and for the devising of materials geared to local educational needs, and are making efforts to see that this is the case.

Various Caribbean Member States are making special efforts to expand and diversify their secondary education. The Governments of Barbados, Guyana, Jamaica, and Trinidad and Tobago in particular have ruled that the post-primary sections of all-age schools are to be counted as secondary departments, thus increasing enrolment at this level. This objective calls for a considerable effort to supply the plant, teachers and equipment needed to ensure that the education provided in these departments is genuinely comparable with that provided in other secondary education establishments in the same countries. As a result of these efforts, courses of study are being diversified in a way that meets the requirements of development, mainly by means of comprehensive schools offering various options to pupils.

In the case of Guyana, the programme of the community high schools envisages that students in their final two years will engage in work related to their area of vocational choice. During the early years of the course pre-vocational activities related to the needs of the community in which the school is situated are carried out. One of the major preoccupations of the Government of Trinidad and Tobago is the industrialization of the economy. Since the discovery of large petroleum and natural-gas deposits, its educational plans for the end of the present decade include an integrated programme embracing academic, pre-technician and craft training, utilizing common facilities and with common management, with the object of overcoming the isolation of vocational education from the traditional academic programme. Curriculum reform emphasizes the strengthening of vocational and technical education. In order to co-ordinate these activities and to carry out scientific and technological research programmes, the government has set up a national network of research, development and training institutes, linked together through the National Institute of Higher Education (Research, Science and Technology) (NIHERST).

Suriname has included in its plans the establishment of a general vocational training system at the secondary level, in order to prepare the young people of the country for work. In Jamaica's new secondary schools two years have been added to the programme in order to encourage the teaching of vocational subjects. Dominica, for its part, has set up a technical college to meet the need for more highly skilled workers and to develop its programme for the overall improvement of mathematics and science teaching. Barbados and Guyana are also making special efforts to expand and diversify their vocational and technical education. In Saint Lucia, a curriculum development unit is paying special attention to the improvement of mathematics teaching and to curriculum changes which will help to prepare young people more effectively for employment.

The University of the West Indies (UWI) and the Universities of Guyana and Suriname provide educational opportunities at the third level. The first of these bodies caters for the whole island community of the subregion and is divided into three branches, Mona (Jamaica), St Augustine (Trinidad and Tobago) and Cave Hill (Barbados). In each of the English-speaking Caribbean States, the Department of Extra-Mural Studies of the UWI is represented by a resident tutor and a university centre. To begin with, Guyana used the services of the UWI, but in 1963 it broke away and founded its own university. This is gradually developing into an institution primarily concerned with developing programmes that are geared to the circumstances and needs of the subregion. The University of Suriname, founded in 1968, comprises Faculties of Law, Medicine, Social Sciences and Economics, Natural Sciences and Engineering. It is expected to play an increasing part in the development of national education.

Administration and financing

Administration

The spectacular upsurge in the demand for education, which has exceeded all forecasts in recent years, has forced administrators to introduce stop-gap measures to meet new requirements. Moreover, the new and serious problems confronting them have led to the consideration of the need for reorganizing educational administration.

Their concern with these questions has resulted in a number of important reforms and various studies on this subject. One of the most significant of these studies is *Problemas y tendencias de la administración educacional en América Latina y el Caribe*, published in 1977 by Unesco's Regional Office for Education in Latin America and the Caribbean.

The reforms have borne upon the three main levels of educational administration: (a) the central level, which is the sphere of action of the ministries of education; (b) the intermediate level, composed of regional agencies (or state agencies in federative countries) and provincial, departmental and area agencies; and (c) the institutional level, which covers educational establishments ranging from one-teacher rural schools to institutions of higher education.

The main objectives of the administrative reforms are decentralization, the introduction of technology into the various services and the elimination of excessive bureaucracy. There is broad general agreement in theoretical terms with the need for decentralization, and various statements have been made to that effect, but in practice it is still held up by an unwillingness to hand over decision-making powers or control at certain levels. Furthermore, in the central organization there is a conflict between two basically opposing parties: one holds that the administration should be seen in terms of levels and forms of education, the other favours a horizontal system, in which certain services, such as those concerned with personnel, school buildings and financing, operate jointly at the different educational levels. While the first certainly has some disadvantages, the second puts greater emphasis on formal and administrative procedures, and so loses sight of the fact that educational management is fundamentally the management of educational institutions and not merely of financial and administrative affairs. If this is forgotten, there is a danger that administration will cease to be a means of controlling and developing education systems and become an end in itself.

As regards the types of personnel working in educational administration, the tendency is to enlist the servicies of new specialists, each working in a different field. An efficient modern administration calls for an interdisciplinary approach and new types of professionals. In addition to educators, of course, it should include planning, supervision and evaluation specialists, curriculum specialists, specialists in the economics of education, research specialists, guidance specialists, psychologists, sociologists, etc.

Amongst these professionals, it seems that inadequate attention is being paid to the training and selection of supervisors, whether they are the traditional 'school inspectors' or school principals. It is obvious that persons occupying either of these positions should have a higher level of education than their subordinates and a specialized knowledge of the various techniques involved in the performance of their own duties. Inspectors play a vitally important part in educational administration, performing a fundamental role in the implementation of educational legislation, the study of educational needs within their districts, the evaluation of the efficiency of teachers and educational establishments, and the provision of in-service training for teachers. It goes without saying that the performance of such duties calls for professional training of a very high standard and that unqualified persons should not be appointed to the inspectorate for political or other reasons, as unfortunately happens in many instances.

It is generally acknowledged that Latin America and the Caribbean are in the forefront of other regions in educational planning. All the ministries of education have some kind of planning service. The international agencies have provided special support for the training of educational planners. In this connection, mention may be made of the systematic activities carried out jointly by Unesco and ECLA's Economic and Social Planning Institute. The tasks and responsibilities assigned to the planning services vary considerably from country to country. In certain cases, their role is extremely limited, consisting mainly of the preparation of statistics and quantitative planning. But other planning services are given a considerable degree of responsibility for quantitative and qualitative analyses of education and for the control and evaluation of the implementation of educational plans, and they maintain close links with national economic and social planning agencies.

The countries of the region have been stepping up their efforts to include in their development policies and plans activities designed to preserve their cultural heritage and values, promote artistic creativity and bring about the democratization of culture. Most countries have established or strengthened agencies whose task it is to plan, co-ordinate and carry out cultural activities. Cultural policies are currently being drawn up in several countries, and some have adopted legislative provisions and regulations on literary and artistic property and the protection of the cultural heritage. However, the limited financial resources available for the promotion of cultural development and the lack of co-ordination of the activities conducted by the different bodies or groups undertaking such work place severe limitations on the efforts being made.

Financing

The total financing resources earmarked for education in the region cannot be determined, as full information is not available. Only the public sector's school expenditure on education is recorded with any degree of precision in national statistics.

In most Latin American countries, whether they have centralized or decentralized political and administrative systems, the highest proportion of the resources available for education is provided by the central national administration, although in some countries large amounts are contributed by states, provinces and municipalities.

In all systems, operating or recurrent costs account for the highest proportion of expenditure, close to and sometimes exceeding 90 per cent, while capital investment is relatively low. The greater part of operating costs is represented by the salaries and fees paid to the teaching and administrative staff. Smaller amounts are allocated to the purchase of the necessary supplies, the maintenance and repair of equipment and buildings and social expenditure on behalf of students and staff. Of the total educational outlay in the region, over two-thirds is devoted to recurrent expenditure, while one-fifth consists of grants to educational and scientific institutions; a relatively small amount, approximately one-seventh, is invested.

Throughout the region as a whole, public expenditure on education, as reflected in the budgetary allocations for this sector, amounted to a total of $5,326 million in 1970. This figure rose to $13,654 million in 1976, so that educational expenditure more than doubled in the first six years of the last decade. Moreover, recent figures for public spending on education could be lower than actual expenditure, since in many cases they do not include certain sums allocated by governments mainly to vocational training and other types of non-formal education. The growth rate for public spending on education remained constant up to the middle of the present decade, though there were annual fluctuations.

In the region as a whole, the public sector was devoting 13 per cent of its annual budget to education in the mid-1970s. The situation, however, varies considerably from country to country. In twelve of the twenty-two countries for which data are available, educational expenditure accounts for less than 15 per cent of the national budget, while in five countries the figure lies between 15 and 20 per cent; the other five countries devote more than 20 per cent of their national budget to education, though the figure of 30 per cent is rarely exceeded. For the region as a whole, the trend in the last few years has been towards a decline in the proportion of the national budget devoted to public expenditure on education.

The recommendation made by the Conference on Education and Economic and Social Development in Latin America (Santiago, Chile, 1962) that as from 1965 the region as a whole should devote not less than 4 per cent of its gross product to education has not been put into effect. Around 1976, fourteen years after the Declaration of Santiago, the proportion of gross national product (GNP) devoted to public expenditure on education came to an average of 3.4 per cent for twenty-eight countries of the region. This average, however, conceals wide variations between countries. One group, which includes Barbados, Costa Rica, Cuba, Guyana, Jamaica, St Vincent and Saint Lucia, devoted more than 6 per cent of their GNP to education in that year. A second group, which includes Antigua, Ecuador, Grenada, Honduras, Mexico, Panama, St Kitts-Nevis-Anguilla, Suriname and Venezuela, earmarked a proportion ranging from 4 to 5.9 per cent for education, while a third group, consisting of Bolivia, Chile, El Salvador, Peru, and Trinidad and Tobago, allocated a proportion ranging from 3.4 to 3.8 per cent. In the seven remaining countries, the proportion varied from 0.9 to 2.8 per cent.

Between 1970 and 1976 public expenditure on education per pupil rose in twenty-six of the twenty-eight countries, though the range of difference in this indicator is very wide. In 1976, for instance, Venezuela had the highest expenditure, with $526 a year, and Haiti the lowest, with $15.

Part Two

Outline of the present educational situation

Factors affecting the situation

Demographic factors

Despite some evidence of downward trends, the population continues to increase at a cumulative annual rate of 2.7 per cent. The total population in the region rose from 212 million in 1960 to 279 million in 1970 and to 320 million in 1975. According to estimates of the United Nations Population Division, it will reach the 421-million mark by 1985 and 614 million by the year 2000. This growth rate, however, has not been consistent throughout the region. One group of countries, comprising Argentina, Barbados, Chile, Cuba, Dominica, Grenada, Haiti, Jamaica, Montserrat, St Kitts-Nevis-Anguilla, Saint Lucia, St Vincent, Trinidad and Tobago, and Uruguay, has at present an average annual growth rate of 2 per cent or less, while another group, consisting of Bolivia, Brazil, Colombia, Costa Rica, Dominican Republic, Ecuador, El Salvador, Guatemala, Guyana, Honduras, Mexico, Nicaragua, Panama, Paraguay, Peru, Suriname and Venezuela, shows growth rates varying between 2 and 3 per cent.

In most countries the drop in mortality rates and high birth-rates have combined to produce a population age-structure in which children and young people predominate. In 1970 the 0-to-24-year age-group accounted for 62 per cent and the 5-to-24-year age-group for 45 per cent of the population. The 5-to-14-year age-group, which covers the years of basic education, rose from 54 million in 1960 to 83 million in 1975 and will reach 106 million by 1985.

During the last decade there has been a slight drop in birth-rates, and according to the projections of the Latin American Demographic Centre (CELADE), it is anticipated that this will lead to an increasingly rapid decline in the average annual population growth rate in the next two decades, from 2.8 per cent in 1970–75 to less than 2.6 per cent by the turn of the century. But even with this drop and the fall in infant mortality rates, the population growth rate for the region will be higher than the rate forecast for the world population.

There have been far-reaching changes in the geographical distribution of the population of the region. Over the period in question, the concentration of the population in urban areas, chiefly in the major cities, has continued and has exacerbated the problems of overcrowding, environmental pollution, labour-market distortions, failure to meet the demand for services, cultural maladjustment of immigrants, and so on. Less than half the population of Latin America lives outside urban areas. This situation also applies in the more densely populated countries of the Caribbean. However, a distinction has to be made between various levels of urban concentration. In four countries (Argentina, Chile, Uruguay and Venezuela), 70 per cent of the population or more live in urban areas; in nine others (Barbados, Brazil, Colombia, Cuba, Jamaica, Mexico, Nicaragua, Panama and Peru) this percentage is between 70 and 45 per cent. In a third group, composed of eleven countries (Antigua, Bolivia, Costa Rica, the Dominican Republic, El Salvador, Ecuador, Guatemala, Guyana, Paraguay, St Kitts-Nevis-Anguilla and Suriname), the urban population is somewhat more than a third of the total population, while in three others (Haiti, Honduras, and Trinidad and Tobago) city-dwellers account for slightly more than 20 per cent of the total.

As far as the Caribbean is concerned, the distinction between the urban and rural categories is not so clear-cut. These categories are applicable to some of the countries in the subregion, but in others the similarity of life-style makes it inappropriate to use the criteria for urban–rural division that are generally applied in the region.

In spite of migration from the countryside to the cities, the rural population continues to grow in absolute terms. In the changing geographical distribution pattern of this rural population there are, furthermore, two features which are of obvious significance as far as education is concerned. These are the continued existence of small, scattered communities, and the size of the migrant groups in search of work opportunities.

In conclusion, if the current trends continue, the population of the region at the end of the decade 1980–90 will amount to almost 486 million people, of whom 70 per cent will be living in cities. Even in the least urbanized countries, city-dwellers will outnumber the inhabitants of rural areas. As a consequence of the population growth rates and the age structure, the active population will increase at an annual rate of close on 3 per cent, which will present a challenge to the economies of the region in terms of their capacity to absorb the labour force. The 15-to-64-year age-group will increase from 171 million to 353 million over the next twenty-five years.

This picture of the demographic situation has a number of important implications for the education systems. The under-fifteens represented 42 per cent of the total population in 1970. There was an increase in population density but, in most countries, the average density did not exceed thirty inhabitants per square kilometre, as the high concentration in a few areas was offset by the sparse population throughout the rest of the country. The demand for education and training is more than likely to increase, and this will put pressure on the various levels of the education system in both quantitative and qualitative terms, leading to the introduction of new goals and structural diversification in education. Urbanization will have a variety of effects. On the one hand, it is more than likely that there will be an increase in the demand for all sorts of goods and services, in the pressure on the physical and social infrastructure in urban areas, with the consequent changes in social stratification in both rural and urban areas, and in the problems connected with integrating the migrants into urban society. On the other hand, city life will continue to influence the mentality and aspirations of the migrants, for it will expose them to new ways of thinking, the mass media, a vast quantity of information and an abundance of interpersonal relations which will alter their perception of social space and time.

Until now, the urban sectors of the population in most countries of the region have demanded and obtained a favourable allocation of resources for a full range of education and training. This situation serves to make the cities more attractive to rural migrants. The continued or increased dispersion of the rural population has led to a rise in the unit cost of its education, but most of the countries in the region have failed to effect improvements in teaching methods, curricula or school organization which would make it possible to avoid the growing discrimination against the rural population.

The educational implications of demographic patterns and trends are not difficult to see. Owing to the rapid growth of the population, which is composed of an increasingly large proportion of children and young people, the countries of the region have had to make a tremendous effort to expand and finance their education systems. The considerable increase in enrolments at the different educational levels, which has already been described, points to the highly satisfactory quantitative results that have been achieved, although improvements in the quality of education have not kept pace with the rate of expansion, owing to the makeshift nature of the measures it was necessary to adopt in providing personnel and materials and the lack of financial resources to meet the new requirements satisfactorily.

Socio-economic factors

The salient features of economic growth over the last two decades have been analysed by ECLA. It distinguishes various stages since 1950. The initial stage, covering the period up to the mid-1960s, showed a moderate but constant annual growth rate of just over 5 per cent. The pace of growth quickened in the 1965–74 period; the average annual increase in gross domestic product (GDP) was 6.7 per cent, rising to 7.5 per cent in the first four years of the decade. Domestic demand grew considerably, while exports were increased and diversified. The real value of exports went up and improvements were made in institutional structures and in economic organization and planning.

In 1974, just at the time when the economic growth rate of the industrialized countries showed a marked decline, the economic outlook in the region began to undergo a radical change. The countries in the region—apart from the oil-exporting countries—experienced a drastic drop in the economic growth rate, which stood at a mere 2.9 per cent in 1975. There were several reasons for this: the falling off in foreign demand, the drop in raw material prices, the effects of inflation on the prices of imported products and, obviously, the new oil prices.

The year 1976 saw the start of a process of recovery which is still continuing. However, it has been a moderate recovery, with an average annual growth rate in the last four years of 4.5 per cent for the whole region; 4 per cent if the oil-exporting countries are excluded. This whole process has revealed the extreme vulnerability of the economies in the region and their sensitivity to world economic trends and, more particularly, to the growth rate of the industrialized countries. On the other hand, during the 1970s the disparities and gaps between the different countries of the region became more marked, on account of differences in population numbers and domestic markets, in the availability of natural resources and in the ability of management to organize production and produce policies to cope with the adverse factors resulting from the world economic situation. In recent years, consideration has been given to the possibility of classifying countries as net petroleum exporters and net petroleum importers. Bolivia, Colombia, Ecuador, Mexico, Trinidad and Tobago, and Venezuela come into the first category, and the other countries of the region into the second.

The economy of the English-speaking countries of the Caribbean is mainly based on the export of plantation products and mineral raw materials and, more recently and to a lesser extent, on tourism. Their industrialization processes have been established only recently, and they are slow and largely tied to the interests of the transnational corporations. This makes it necessary for them to import machinery and foodstuffs, and produces an unfavourable balance of payments (except in the case of Trinidad and Tobago) with consequent serious problems of unemployment and underemployment.

The structure of production in the region has undergone marked changes; there has been a decline in agricultural and mining activities and an increase in activities connected with manufacturing and construction, trade, finance, administration, services and so on. Over the past three decades the region has changed from an agricultural to a semi-industrialized society.

With regard to agriculture (including forestry, hunting and fisheries), if we look at the figures since 1950—when this sector accounted for 20 per cent of the regional product—we shall see that there has been a constant decline in its relative share of the national product. In 1960 it generated 17.1 per cent of the national product, whereas the proportion had fallen to 13.3 per cent by 1970 and a bare 11.6 per cent in 1975. Up to the time of writing, in the 1970s, however, agricultural and livestock production has increased in constant absolute terms. Even so, there has been no real rise in per capita output, since the growth rate has merely kept pace with population increase.

The sector with the region's fastest growth rate was the industrial sector. The average annual growth rate constantly stood at over 6 per cent and, with the exception of 1974, was higher than the growth rate of GDP. However, the growth of this sector has not lived up to the hopes placed in it by optimistic forecasts, which regarded it as being the decisive factor in the socio-economic transformation of the region and in the increased ability of its economies to provide employment for the population. Industrial progress came about mainly as a result of the direct incorporation of expensive foreign technologies and the participation—often predominantly—of the transnational corporations. At the same time, industrial development in the region is characterized by the existence side by side of industry employing advanced technology and a traditional sector composed of medium, small and craft enterprises with low productivity. This traditional sector is the larger, both in the number of enterprises and in the volume of labour. The same situation can be seen in the agricultural sector.

The Chaguaramas Evaluation (Trinidad and Tobago, 1975) summed up the unequal distribution of income in the following terms:

After more than a decade in which national policies have tried to obtain a more equitable distribution of income, in Latin America it continues to be more concentrated than in most parts of the world, and the gap between those groups nearer to the top level of income and those at the bottom has widened. The extraordinarily unequal distribution of income and the persistence of massive poverty derive, partly, from the distribution of power in societies and, partly, from a style of dominant development unable to incorporate the greater part of the rapidly growing manpower in sufficiently productive occupations or in those having sufficient social demand so as to offer adequate incomes.

A recent ECLA survey covering 70 per cent of the population of Latin America confirms these statements by statistics indicating that 60 per cent of the increase in per capita income between 1960 and 1970 went to 20 per cent of the population, who formed the most prosperous and socially privileged group. During that decade, 40 per cent of the population managed to increase their annual income by no more than $20. The diversity already existing in the structure of production is found to an even greater extent if one compares the different economic branches, the regions in each country, and the countries themselves.

The process of technological modernization has not taken place in the under-capitalized or weak sectors of the economy, but in those urban and rural activities where productivity was already up to the average. Technical progress, with its consequential impact on consumption and incomes, is not to be found everywhere in the region; it is highly concentrated, and this affects the structure of employment and the distribution of incomes and consumption.

Economic growth is concentrated in certain key activities, the chief of these being the production of durable consumer goods and, to some extent, the manufacture of capital goods and the provision of services. An analysis of the pattern of foreign investment shows that it is focused on these same high-productivity activities. Thus the ties of dependency that existed in the different stages of the region's history are now being tightened further by the growing impact of foreign firms and transnational corporations and the control they exercise in these industrial sectors, in the exploitation of the natural resources that are the staple export commodity of some countries, and in essential public utilities and the commercial, banking and financial system. The situation of some Caribbean countries regarding the sugar industry is a further example of this. Despite the fact that there has been some nationalization in the oil and mining sectors, dependence on foreign capital investment has continued to increase.[1]

To summarize, as the Chaguaramas Evaluation puts it, the prevailing style of development with its structural diversity has made improvements possible in some aspects of living conditions, but at the same time income disparities have become more marked, and there has been no significant improvement in consumption in such fundamental areas as food and housing, while the economies are as incapable as ever they were of providing productive and well-paid employment.

Successive evaluations of the International Development Strategy carried out by the governments of the countries in the region within the context of ECLA (Quito, 1973; Chaguaramas, Trinidad and Tobago, 1975; Guatemala, 1977; La Paz, 1978) have clearly revealed the structural limitations, inconsistencies and weaknesses of development and, more especially, the limited social impact of economic growth. According to these evaluations, the growth of the economic variables in the region has not produced qualitative changes of any significance as far as human well-being and social justice are concerned. The continued existence of widespread poverty, the inability of the production system to absorb the growing labour potential, the inequalities of income distribution, the fact that large sectors of the population play no part in economic, social and civic life, and the consolidation of consumer patterns that are not related to the needs of the majority are all evidence of the lack of drive and the structural weaknesses of socio-economic development in the region.

One of the points on which analysts of national and regional development have focused their attention is the poverty that characterizes the lives of large sectors of society in the region. Its manifestations are: malnutrition; precarious health, hygiene and housing conditions; the absence, or low standards, of education; under-consumption; lack of organization; and, consequently, social exclusion in the different sectors of the economy. The privations from which these sectors suffer are material—the lack of basic needs—and also psychological, social and political.

The research project on the measurement and analysis of income distribution in Latin American countries carried out by ECLA shows that 40 per cent of Latin American households live in poverty because they are unable to acquire the minimum amount of goods to meet their basic needs. Of the total households, 20 per cent can be said to be living in destitution, in that they have not even the wherewithal to acquire the foodstuffs which would provide them with the minimum level of subsistence. These are, of course, average figures,

---

1. Laurence D. Carrington, *Education and Development in the English-Speaking Caribbean: A Contemporary Survey*, Buenos Aires, ECLA, October 1978. (Unesco/ECLA/UNDP Project 'Development and Education in Latin America and the Caribbean'.) [Doc. DEALC/16.]

the differences between countries being considerable. Nevertheless, it can be stated that as a general rule the situation in rural areas is particularly serious. In the ten countries analysed, it is estimated that 62 per cent of households are below the poverty-line in rural areas and 26 per cent in urban areas; households below the destitution level are estimated at 34 per cent in rural areas and 10 per cent in urban areas.[1]

These social and economic disparities have far-reaching implications with regard to the opportunities for access to education. In his Address to the Sovereign Congress of Oaxaca, given when he inaugurated the congress in 1848, Benito Juárez dwelt upon the close relationship between education and social development. The great Mexican leader put forward the view that

a man who cannot feed his family sees his children's education as something quite irrelevant or as an obstacle to earning a livelihood. Instead of sending them to school, he makes them work in the house or hires out their feeble labour so as to relieve his poverty a little. If this man's circumstances improved, if his daily work brought him some profit, he would see to it that his children were educated and given sound instruction in one of the branches of knowledge. The desire for knowledge and learning is an innate human quality. Free man from the obstacles which poverty and despotism place in his way, and he will learn as a matter of course, even when he is not given any direct support.[2]

Latin American history has always been marked by a concern for education. Education was championed by such liberators as Miranda, Bolívar, San Martín and Hidalgo, and by great thinkers and educators like Sarmiento, Bello, Martí and Varela.

Today education is seen as a fundamental human right, since it is a prerequisite for the development of man's intellectual and spiritual powers and is essential to the proper exercise of his other rights and duties. Through education, society transmits its norms and values; this is how the social system is reproduced.

While cultural inequality will occur in any system where there is stratification, education is one of the mechanisms that can contribute to the creation of equal social opportunities for each new generation.

Education is subject, as never before, to new pressures and demands from the societies in which it is provided. These increased requirements, which put a heavy load on education systems and frequently necessitate education reforms, primarily stem from rapid social development and the growing aspirations of the people to improve their position and their well-being in personal and occupational terms. They feel that they will not realize their aspirations without firm and effective action on the part of educational institutions. Any study of the main factors of the social pressure to which education is subject today will recognize the importance of demographic, economic and social factors and those arising out of scientific and technological progress. In Latin

1. Oscar Altimir, *La dimensión de la pobreza en América Latina*, Santiago de Chile, United Nations Economic Commission for Latin America (ECLA), September 1978.
2. Benito Juárez, *Documentos, discursos, correspondencia*, Vol. 1, pp. 561–2, (Selection and notes by Jorge L. Tamayo), Mexico City, Secretaría del Patrimonio Nacional, 1971.

America and the Caribbean, such factors, which are today found in all societies, take on the particular features that we have described. The most serious educational situation is found in rural areas, where poverty is greatest. It is known that an inadequate diet impairs intellectual development and efficiency at school. Furthermore, the practice of putting very young children to work in rural areas is responsible for the high drop-out rates which, in turn, account for the high illiteracy rates.

Although the expansion of the education systems has led to a significant increase in the figures for access to secondary and higher education, the pattern of the social origins of the students, particularly of university students, has not altered appreciably in favour of the underprivileged social classes.

The main problems

The crisis in education systems

Never before have education systems expanded on such a scale as they have today. Never before has such a variety of opportunities been available to young people. Yet, in the past, dissatisfaction with education never reached the level it has today. Adverse criticism of education was indeed voiced in bygone days, even in the time of Socrates, but it was never as intense and as sweeping as it is today.

Over the past two decades, education systems have received much harsh criticism from a variety of quarters: criticism of education in itself, educational content and teaching methods. Strangely enough, in recent years the most radical attacks on educational institutions in the official education system—on the school—have been made in Latin America. The Centre for Intercultural Documentation (CIDOC) in Cuernavaca (Mexico), with which Ivan Illich and Everett Reimer are associated, embodies the most outspoken anti-school trend.

In his grimly entitled book, *School is Dead*,[1] Reimer, who is a close associate of Ivan Illich, relentlessly calls the school to account. His criticism is conducted on three levels: (a) an analysis of the economic problems brought about by the present education system; (b) a study of the nature and role of institutions in post-industrial society; and (c) a serious appraisal of the psychological and educational assumptions underlying the school as an educational structure.

In Reimer's view, the greatest danger facing mankind is the total domination of individuals by institutions. In any economic and political system, man is now a mere cog in a gigantic machine built to produce goods for consumption and controlled by a privileged minority. This progressive change robs man of his most precious gifts, namely his freedom, his spontaneity and

---

1. E. W. Reimer, *School is Dead*, Harmondsworth, Penguin Books, 1971.

his creativity. According to Reimer, the school has to shoulder its full share of blame for this situation, because it confers a social status and selects the rulers and the ruled, with a view to their integration in an excessively hierarchic society based on individual ability. But—still more serious—the school trains the pupil to defer to all the other institutions in society. The educational monopoly is simply one aspect of the monopoly of technology, for in the logic of technology everyone, whether he is a chief or a subordinate, has to be moulded by the school system, so as to fit into the pattern of competitive consumption. The conclusion is simply this: if we wish to free man from technological domination, we must start by destroying the school.

The reader is struck at the outset by the fact that Reimer's criticism of schools is completely abstract; it is historical and purely formal. The difference, for example, between the kind of school that existed in Nazi Germany and Freinet's school is so vast that it is impossible to make a judgement on schools without analysing a specific situation. The view that school is synonymous with 'militarization' and kills off spontaneity and creativity is, strictly speaking, meaningless, since the author sidesteps the fundamental question, namely whether it is the school itself or the conception of the school in certain political systems that justifies the overall analysis. When such a fundamental institution is being discussed, we are entitled to demand a minimum of methodological accuracy. Reimer sees the school as the agency that determines the way in which contemporary society functions. In broader terms, he takes the view that society is no more than a reflection of its educational institutions. In these assumptions the real ties of dependence between school and the outside world are completely reversed. Inequalities and social classes are not created by the school alone. They are created by the economic system. The school merely reflects and in some degree perpetuates this system, for it also has unquestionably an influence on social change.

The school is not neutral. As a means of socialization—and, consequently, a means of assimilating certain cultural norms, a certain system of values—the school fashions (or tries to fashion) people in the image of a society. This being the case, the question can no longer be considered in relation to school as such; it has to be considered in terms of the various political models of a specific society.

To see individuals in opposition to institutions is to create a false problem. Reimer merely reverts to an oversimplified Rousseauism. The real question is: 'Who controls these institutions and what interests do they represent?'

This superficial view of the relations between society and institutions is combined with an extremely questionable conception of history: according to Reimer, the cause of all our ills is the development of science and technology; individuals are uprooted from their natural environment and subjected to the ruthless logic of the cycle of production and consumption. A large proportion of the population is undoubtedly excluded from decision-making and planning bodies, and has no direct means of exerting any real control over economic development and bringing it into line with genuine human needs. But this is a matter of social structure, not of development as such. It is paradoxical that

Reimer can censure this phenomenon at a time when technical discoveries and the expansion of the productive forces will make it possible, through the transformation of the relations of production, to free millions of people in Third World countries from alienating, exhausting jobs and from being engrossed in the daily struggle for survival.

Illich's thought has developed along similar lines. The titles of some of his works speak for themselves: 'School, This Sacred Cow' (published in No. 280 of *Les temps modernes*), *La futilidad de la escuela en América Latina*. Illich sees the school as a paradigm of a disastrous institutionalization of values which imposed 'consumerism' and creates divisions between the pupils, who are the prisoners of the educational structure. He also holds the view that everyone learns to live, speak, think, love, feel, develop and work outside school. In *Deschooling Society*[1] he proposes the creation of a flexible web in which anyone who wants to learn can have access to the resources and contacts needed to further his own development. For this purpose he conceives four networks. The first would give the public access to 'educational objects'; the second would be a 'skill-exchange service'; the third would facilitate 'peer-matching'; the fourth would provide an up-to-date list of 'educators-at-large'. Needless to say, this proposal implies the abolition of school, which would be replaced by other types of educational institution.

There is no point in denying that some of the criticisms of the school are justified or that the ideas prompted by such analyses—that routine should be abolished and that educational institutions need renewing and improving—are good ideas. But it is obvious that this view has its share of unfair judgements and errors and an undeniable touch of utopianism.

It is inadmissible to overlook the contribution made by schools and other educational institutions to the progress and well-being of man. The gigantic advances in science, culture and technology, which have improved man's work, health, living standards and nutrition in so many ways, were not achieved by illiterates or autodidacts. They were brought about by generations of former students of these educational institutions, particularly institutions of higher education.

An oddly conservative view of education is discernible in the work of both Illich and Reimer. They seem to imply that 'independent' learning is the fundamental aspect of education. It goes without saying that, in education, book-learning with its limitations is far less important than the cultivation of logical, abstract thought, the learning of methods of work (including, naturally, intellectual work) and, above all, the all-round and harmonious development of the pupil's personality. But such an approach is only possible within a human and material framework (teacher and school) in which the educational process keeps pace with the psychological development of the pupil. Reimer gives no answer on this fundamental issue: for him, the child is not to be guided by competent teachers during the course of his education: he

1. Ivan Illich, *Deschooling Society*, New York, Harper & Row, 1971.

should be at complete liberty to begin his education at the age of 20 if he so wishes, that is, after irretrievably throwing away the best years for intellectual development. In practical terms, how could the new institutions proposed by Illich be established outside the major centres of population? And, lastly, if compulsory schooling were abolished, would there not be a great risk that the children of financially disadvantaged families or those from a rural environment would completely drop out of school, thus exacerbating the present inequality of educational opportunity?

Other critics base their arguments on what they see as a split between school and society. They accuse the school of being unaware of people's needs, and claim that this lack of awareness impairs their ability to train the professionals and labour force needed by the economy. This line of argument is pursued in P. H. Coombs's well-known work *The World Educational Crisis*[1] and in Pierre Jaccard's *Politique de l'emploi et de l'éducation*.[2] A view diametrically opposed to that just described is held by various extreme left-wing groups who take the view that the school's total subordination to capitalist society is the root cause of alienation.

Certain writers attribute the crisis to educational content. It is maintained that education is often quite unrelated to the pupils' interests. This is said to explain their indifference or boredom and their increasingly hostile attitude to curricula which, so far as they can see, do not match their abilities or aspirations. Such writers consider that the basic problem is concerned with objectives, values and content. The fact that curricula are often encyclopedic in nature has been repeatedly criticized by teachers, parents and students themselves, more and more of whom question the relevance, usefulness and educational value of much of the knowledge that such curricula demand. In addition, curricula are generally uniform and compulsory, and this, combined with excessive control over educational activities, gives educational establishments and teachers little scope or encouragement for adapting the learning process to the aptitudes, interests and learning-pace of students, and to regional and local conditions. In these circumstances, teachers concentrate on meeting the formal requirements of the curriculum, with emphasis on the expository method and memorization, and on preparation for tests and examinations, losing sight of the educational values and aims for the achievement of which the curriculum should simply serve as a means.

It is said jokingly that teachers are more progressive in politics than in education. This is particularly true in regard to teaching methods, for there is a tendency to use only such methods as do not require any pupil participation. This problem is fairly widespread, although we are unaware that any research on the subject has been conducted in the region.

The findings of a survey carried out by the French National Commission

1. P. H. Coombs, *The World Educational Crisis: A Systems Analysis*, New York, Oxford University Press, 1968.
2. Pierre Jaccard, *Politique de l'emploi et de l'éducation*, Paris, Payot, 1957.

for co-operation with Unesco may, *mutatis mutandis*, serve to illustrate the point in question. The survey sample was composed of 1,000 teachers. One of the questions asked was whether they used activity methods. Some 17 per cent of the respondents stated that they always used such methods, 78 per cent used them occasionally and 5 per cent never used them. It is interesting to note, however, that out of the 95 per cent of teachers who stated that they always or occasionally used activity methods, only 38 per cent regarded them as wholly satisfactory. The other 62 per cent had doubts about their real effectiveness.

The most important factor in the effectiveness of education is the level and quality of teacher-training. The region has not yet solved the problem of the increased number of teachers who have not received any regular or systematic teacher-training. This state of affairs has come about largely as a result of the rapid and very substantial expansion of the systems of education, which has made it necessary to engage the services of such personnel.

However, there is not always an actual shortage of qualified personnel, or at least not as great a shortage as this situation would suggest. Many qualified teachers choose other employment, some working outside the education sector, attracted as they are by higher earnings, better career prospects and greater security. There still seems to be a tendency for graduates to refuse posts in rural areas, in small towns and even in outlying districts of large towns and cities. In some cases, this tendency is becoming more marked.

Pay conditions, which are unsatisfactory in a good number of countries, also have an adverse effect on the recruitment and efficiency of teachers. When combined with the fact that teachers do not always take part in the development of reforms, this situation tends to make teachers sceptical about the wisdom and advisability of such reforms, with the result that their implementation is impaired and a rift or split develops between teachers and educational administrators.

Mention has already been made of one very eloquent indicator of the poor level of efficiency in education systems: the high percentage of school drop-outs and the growing number of repeaters. It would seem that insufficient attention is being given to support activities and measures to prevent pupils from dropping out, which would undoubtedly improve the situation. This is particularly important in cases where pupils have not had any pre-school education or where they come from a family environment providing little cultural stimulation and are thereby at a considerable disadvantage in relation to pupils who are more fortunate in this respect.

Automatic promotion has been tried out in a number of countries as a way of dealing with the problem of repeaters, and has yielded a variety of results. Unless the pupils who are put up without attaining the educational standard required for a given level or phase of education receive additional help with their weak subjects, automatic promotion is of very little benefit to either the pupils concerned or the classes into which they are put without attaining the required standard. Hence the importance of providing special classes or other kinds of help for such pupils, particularly those based on methods of individualized instruction.

Inequality of educational opportunities

The recent celebration of the International Education Year afforded an opportunity to awaken or foster public interest in the major educational issues through lectures, publications and a variety of other activities. The international agencies, particularly the United Nations Children's Fund (UNICEF) and Unesco, as well as numerous countries, have been extremely active in this field. One of the points emphasized has been inequality of educational opportunities, a theme closely linked to that of the right to education.

As is generally known, the principle and recognition of this right is embodied in the Universal Declaration of Human Rights, approved by the General Assembly of the United Nations in 1948. Article 26 of the Declaration states:

Everyone has the right to education. Education shall be free, at least in the elementary and fundamental stages. Elementary education shall be compulsory. Technical and professional education shall be made generally available, and higher education shall be equally accessible to all on the basis of merit.

The various facts and figures relating to educational trends in Latin America and the Caribbean and to the state of education at present show that there is a wide gap between the objectives set forth in the Universal Declaration of Human Rights and the education opportunities available to the population of the region, despite the major advances which have been made. Of course this problem is not peculiar to Latin America and the Caribbean; it affects all countries, and is a matter of concern even to those which have made greater progress in education, since the factors that work against fundamental, real equality of opportunity are extremely varied and will not easily be surmounted by those countries. Yet it is obviously unsatisfactory that the right to equal opportunities should be no more than a mere statement of principles; nor is well-meaning legislation sufficient. The main causes of the present inequalities in education must be analysed, and the most appropriate measures for overcoming them must be studied and put into effect.

But how is the concept of equality in education to be defined? In his work *Para una igualdad de oportunidades*,[1] T. Husén distinguishes three main phases in the evolution of this concept, which have always coexisted although they were recognized successively:

The conservative phase. According to Husén, this phase predominated up to the First World War in industrialized countries, and was characterized, in ideological terms, by a philosophy that asserted that God has endowed each man with different gifts which he has to put to the best possible use. According to the most reactionary version of this philosophy, the abilities of each person correspond to his social class, and he should therefore be content with his position in society.

1. T. Husén, *Para una igualdad de oportunidades*, Madrid, Instituto Calasanz de Ciencias de la Educación (ICCE), 1978.

A less conservative version was based upon the notion of *selectio ingeniorum* (selection of the most gifted) and maintained that highly gifted persons were also to be found among the masses. It was only the need for a skilled labour force that broke the elementary-school/grammar-school pattern and led to the introduction of a shorter form of secondary education which did not prepare students for university.

The liberal phase. Briefly, it may be said that the dominant idea in this phase was that, from the moment of his birth, every man possesses a variety of more or less constant abilities and that the education system should remove all external obstacles to their normal development. This was the idea underlying a number of reforms in the educational structure, such as the introduction of a period of compulsory schooling which was less differentiated and more cohesive. It was thought that a general education and the accessibility of secondary education to children from all social classes would remove all the obstacles encountered by children who were poor or who lived a long way from school. But no account was taken of a number of factors that had already marked the child before the age of pre-school education. Apart from anything else, a child's language ability when he begins school, which depends directly on his family environment and social class, has a decisive effect on his success at school. The school, therefore, cannot of itself iron out differences in school results, the cause of which must be sought in the pupils' economic and social environment.

A new notion of equal educational opportunities

In fact, a good many of the advanced countries have introduced a series of educational reforms which, if we take the most optimistic view of things, will lead to equal educational opportunities in the long run: for example, the one-tier comprehensive systems which replaced the traditional two-tier education systems. The comprehensive system effectively deferred the moment at which the pupil had to make a definitive choice, and in principle reduced inequalities by giving underprivileged pupils the option of completing their secondary education. However, inequality prevails in the long run; it is merely deferred to the pre-university or university level. It was therefore necessary to revise the premises of the liberal belief that the innate abilities of the child would be free to develop if external obstacles were removed. In fact, a broader and less competitive conception has been adopted in advanced countries.

Equality of opportunities accordingly implies that different individuals are treated dissimilarly, for 'equal opportunities' does not mean 'identical opportunities'. Equality of opportunities entails specific forms of assistance for those most in need of it and special attention for those who are psychologically, socially or economically disadvantaged.

Lastly, T. Husén maintains that 'according to the most modern and most radical idea of educational equality, the long-term objective of greater equality in the direction and quality of life calls for a far broader outlook which sets the school in the context of society at large'. Educational reform is no substitute for social reform.

The International Conference on Education organized by Unesco and held in Geneva in 1971 listed the main factors that hamper the general observance of the right to education and, consequently, equality of opportunity. These factors are:

the social structure of societies, the socio-economic characteristics of the environment, the socio-economic background of the pupils (the occupation of parents, family income, living conditions, states of health, etc.);

social and cultural factors (educational standard of parents, cultural level of the environment, mother tongue, the status of ethnic and linguistic minorities, religious beliefs, and influence of certain traditions, etc.);

geographical and demographic factors (place of residence, density of population and its distribution over the territory, density of school network, transport, etc.);

educational factors (structure of the school system, language of instruction, curricula, methods, evaluation and examinations, attitude and competence of teachers, etc.);

the pupil's perception of his place and opportunities in the school system;

the level of psychological development of children.

The above quotation shows that the question of the right to education and the democratization of education extends far beyond the confines of education systems as such and that inequalities in education stem largely from economic and social inequalities.

The *Plowden Report* suggests that size, weight, resistance to illness and maturity vary with socio-economic class. Even in such a comparatively homogeneous country as the United Kingdom, quite significant differences are to be found:

Environmental and hereditary factors interact inextricably to produce these differences between socio-economic classes. One set of factors tends to reinforce, not cancel out, the other. Socio-economic classes are heterogeneous and artificial, and it is not so much the family's occupation or income that is operative here as its attitudes and traditions of child care, its child centredness, its whole cultural outlook. As the more intelligent and forward-looking parent moves up the social scale, so his children's conditions improve: the less intelligent, less ambitious and more passive parent creates conditions which give less stimulation and support to the child's physical development. Similar considerations apply to intellectual development. Intelligent parents, who have themselves gained educational and social advantages, tend to make effective use of the educational, social and medical provision for their children. There is a strong association between the circumstances which affect the nutritional conditions underlying progress in physical development and those other conditions which nourish, as it were, intellectual and emotional growth.

Leaving aside these factors, which are discussed in the section of this work devoted to the economic, social and cultural conditions that affect childhood, we shall consider such questions as fall strictly within the confines of educational psychology and certain trends in educational selection which have become apparent, particularly in recent years.

Looking at the structure of the education systems in the region, we see that little has been done to provide pre-school education. Furthermore, where pre-school education has been introduced, it is not provided for those most in need of it. It is generally unavailable to rural children or to urban children whose families lack the means to send them to the private pre-school centres, which usually make up the bulk of the establishments offering this level of education.

It may be said that this is the child's first experience of educational discrimination, the consequences of which will not easily be repaired later, since the earliest years of a person's life are extremely important for his intellectual development.

The development of the intelligence is largely dependent on the richness and quality of the perceptual and mental stimuli which the child receives in his family. The basic elements of cultural life (books, magazines, newspapers, etc.) are to be found in the houses of the privileged social classes, and the children who belong to those classes receive stimuli that are conducive to their intellectual development and the acquisition of knowledge, as well as their parents' help with their learning. By contrast, the lack of such things in needy households puts the children at a disadvantage, not because they are ungifted, but because they are conditioned by the situation in which they live. This does not mean that a lack of financial resources will necessarily be accompanied by an unstimulating environment. 'Educational deprivation' does not have to result from poverty; education in the home, parental attitudes and motherly care are more important for the child's intellectual development and learning than the actual financial status of the family.

Various research studies have shown the effects of the environment on performance at school; they suggest that, although a deprived socio-cultural environment can account for retardation, it does so to the extent that it hampers the full development of latent abilities. This view is shared by Piaget, who believes that the constant observed in the sequence of the development stages of operative intelligence depends, at least partly, on the biological maturation of the nervous system, while the great variations in the age at which a stage occurs or fails to occur show that maturation is not everything; they highlight the role of the social environment and the education received by the child.

The educational opportunities available to certain sectors of the indigenous population, particularly in Bolivia, Ecuador, Guatemala, Mexico and Peru, are extremely poor in this respect. Although there are similarities in the situation of these sectors, their way of life and problems are not, strictly speaking, comparable. The situation varies—very considerably in some aspects—from one sector of the indigenous population to another. One such aspect, which has a considerable effect on their way of life, is the land-ownership system. In certain countries, agrarian reforms gave broad sectors of the Indian population the opportunity for land-ownership, although such reforms were not always accompanied by the provision of a proper education and agricultural training for the peasants who found themselves in this new situation, as they should have been. In other countries, the latifundiary system continues to prevail and, as a rule, the working conditions of the Indian are extremely harsh and unjust. For instance, some Indians are still paid by having the use of a plot on which they can grow crops to meet their most basic food requirements for part of the year, while they work it to grow crops for the landowner for the rest of the year.

Some degree of progress has been achieved in this matter, mainly because those who experience such living conditions have become aware of the situation and because of the resolute action taken by certain revolutionary or reform movements which have gained the power to make political decisions.

This problem is not peculiar to developing countries; even the most advanced countries are nowhere near achieving the desirable level of equal opportunity. Herbert Gans[1] writes about such a highly developed country as the United States in the following terms:

America can be described as an unequal society that would like to think of itself as egalitarian. While officially dedicated to equality of opportunity, to enabling the disadvantaged to succeed on the basis of their individual ambition and talent, America has not acted to remove the group handicaps—of class, race and sex, among others— which prevent many people from actually realizing that opportunity. Rich and poor, for example, have an equal opportunity to work as common labourers, but the poor rarely obtain the education and social contacts that provide access to executive positions. Equality, therefore, cannot be defined solely in terms of opportunity; it must be judged by results, by whether current inequalities of income and wealth, occupation, political power, and the like are being reduced.

In the case of groups who speak only the vernacular language, and even in that of bilingual groups (vernacular and national languages), the problem of communication is one of the aspects creating most difficulties in education in general, and in literacy and post-literacy training in particular.

This problem also exists, though perhaps not to the same extent, in countries such as Haiti and certain English-speaking countries where the official language is now quite different from the everyday spoken language of the people. Much has been done in the various countries of the region to cater more adequately for the educational needs of these people by taking their specific culture into account.

Examples of such action include the Bilingual Indigenous Extension Worker Programme organized by the Directorate of Rural Social and Educational Development in the Ministry of Education of Guatemala, the establishment, in a rural area of the country, of a teacher-training college given over entirely to the training of indigenous teachers, and the use of textbooks and reading materials in some of the vernacular languages spoken in the country. Another example is the use of vernacular languages in various countries in the Andean area, such as Bolivia, Ecuador and Peru, particularly for literacy training and adult-education programmes and in some cases for primary education as well. In Mexico, under the National Education Plan, education programmes are organized by the Co-ordination Unit for

1. Herbert J. Gans, *More Equality*, New York, Pantheon, 1973.

Educational Services for Deprived Areas and Marginal Groups, which is part of the Secretariat of Public Education. In Haiti, Creole is used in schools; in Paraguay, the ordinary education programmes are adapted to suit the needs of indigenous groups, special courses have been introduced for training indigenous teachers, and the study of Guaraní is compulsory in the first two years of primary education. The legislation of certain countries contains express provisions for such groups, either in respect of literacy training or basic education, or as a reflection of the desire to ensure the preservation of the vernacular languages they use.

However, some points connected with the problem of the use of the vernacular as the language of instruction need to be clarified. Although it is undoubtedly important to use the mother tongue as the medium of instruction, at least in the early grades, with a view to the child's intellectual and emotional development, it has to be admitted that the indigenous peoples themselves are eager for their children to learn the national language, which they consider essential to social advancement. We might recall the words of a petition presented to President Arosemena of the Republic of Ecuador by the leader of an Indian village near Otavalo, which read: 'We want our children to be taught in Spanish so that they can be teachers like other people's children and presidents of the Republic like you.'

Another sector of the population which does not receive adequate educational opportunities, although it has the most need of them, is composed of those people suffering from physical, sensory or mental handicaps. This problem, which is so distressing in human terms, both for the handicapped themselves and for their families, also has an important social dimension in that, with suitable training, many of them could easily be integrated into the environment in which they live. It is not so much a matter of simply providing the basic necessities for each disabled person as of helping him to develop his capabilities to the full. The subnormal suffer from a variety of prejudices arising from ignorance, psychological barriers created by misunderstanding, and a lack of both qualified personnel, centres and materials to give them the special education they need.

At the other end of the scale is the problem of the education of highly gifted children. This area of education continues to be the subject of a heated debate, which has been fuelled in particular by studies in the field of genetic research and is now becoming even more intense. Some people take the view that exceptionally gifted pupils should be educated in ordinary schools. Others think that they should be educated in special institutions where their gifts can be developed to the full. This is a particularly sensitive issue. In some cases, the education of gifted children has been taken to such extremes that it has acquired racial or other morally objectionable overtones, for instance, the experiments aimed at breeding exceptionally gifted persons by using the semen of leading scientists. On the other hand, it is not right to force all children and young people to learn at exactly the same pace. They have different abilities and aptitudes, and any proper interpretation of the aims of education will favour the complete use and development of everyone's potential.

This is a complex problem involving a variety of factors that have to be carefully weighed when we are trying to establish guidelines for its resolution. In the first place, equality of opportunity does not mean that exactly the same levels of performance are sought; that would be unfair towards the individual and also utopian. Second, access to certain phases of education and specialized studies should depend upon people's intellectual ability to undertake them. Scientific and technological progress is largely determined by this factor, since a society needs intellectual élites. At the same time, it is ethically undesirable that the need for such élites should lead to the kind of meritocratic society where overriding importance is attached to intellectual superiority.

The desirability of making the best use of the abilities of talented individuals is today very much a topic of discussion among certain sectors in the most advanced countries, and there is some talk of establishing a 'store' or 'pool' of ability. In the foreword to D. M. McIntosh's book, *Educational Guidance and the Pool of Ability*,[1] it is stated that:

Nations who wish to retain their places in the present ruthless world competition in scientific and other fields must make full use of the resources of talent of their citizens; and for this purpose they will have to take steps to ensure that those who have the ability to come into the pool take advantage of the appropriate educational facilities.

It is worth while recalling that, in the climate of international tension generated by the cold war, particularly in reaction to the 'sputnik shock', talent-scouting became a major national priority. It is symptomatic that the first large-scale United States Federal programme designed to facilitate college access for students from deprived social backgrounds was adopted under the name of the National Defense Education Act of 1958.

The question of selectivity in determining access to certain levels of education is closely related to these issues. It is also discussed from opposing standpoints: one advocating the need for a *numerus clausus* system, the other favouring unrestricted access. The main points in the argument of those holding the first of these views are (a) the need to select the ablest and (b) the employment prospects of pupils. Their opponents maintain that the principle of the democratization of education must be upheld at all costs.

In the foreword to a report published jointly by Unesco and the International Association of Universities,[2] the chairman of the committee set up to assess the project expressed the opinion that an impetus should be given to the expansion of pre-university education, with a view to attracting those who have the necessary abilities:

We should cast our net wider and wider in order to identify, to catch and to bring within the scope of education all available talent, wherever it may be found. This obviously

1. D. M. McIntosh, *Educational Guidance and the Pool of Ability*, p. 6, London, University of London Press, 1959.
2. Joint Unesco-IAU Research Programme in Higher Education, *Access to Higher Education*; Vol. 1: *Director's Report*, by Frank Bowles, p. 15, Paris, Unesco/IAU, 1963.

postulates universal education at the elementary level . . . and the provision of facilities for secondary education of sufficient amplitude to take in as large a proportion as possible of those who finish elementary schools. Out of these we must select those who show promise of being able to meet the intellectual challenge of higher education. In this way, we will be widening the opportunities for higher education but at the same time helping to raise the quality of those who are admitted to it.

The university is accused of preparing generations of students for the 'dole queue'. It is said, in reply, that society, not the university, is responsible for this state of affairs, despite the fact that it needs many trained persons in different fields. Both these standpoints contain elements of truth. To whose advantage is it if hundreds or thousands of graduates in engineering, law, medicine, teaching or other fields, whose training represents a considerable effort on the part of the institutions in which they study and much cost to their families and the state, find themselves unemployed at the end of their course of study? Yet it is undeniable that all countries, particularly developing countries, need a considerably larger body of managers and more professionals and technicians in the different areas of national life than they have at present. Any solution to this predicament must combine efforts to achieve economic and social development with greater rationalization of the procedures and methods of student selection. Development plans, education planning, the establishment of educational and vocational guidance services, and the introduction of scholarships for the most suitable candidates are some of the measures that should be taken with a view to finding the correct solutions to these problems.

Imbalances in the relation between education and employment

The situation

One of the most serious economic and human problems that has to be faced in the region at this time is that of unemployment. It has now attained extraordinary dimensions, as may be seen from Table 14, published by the International Labour Organisation (ILO) on the basis of studies carried out within the framework of the organization's Regional Employment Programme for Latin America and the Caribbean (PREALC).

Unemployment is most heavily concentrated in the 15-to-24-year age-group, i.e. those seeking their first job. The proportion of people in this category who are unemployed and whose skills are therefore wasted is double that of the other age-groups.

According to the definitions given by PREALC, 'equivalent unemployment' means the loss in terms of workers' productive activity because of underemployment, and 'underutilization of the total labour force' means the overall loss arising from open unemployment and equivalent unemployment.

The existence of unemployment is more apparent in the urban areas, but it should not be forgotten that underemployment is high in the rural areas, and

TABLE 14. Summary of the employment situation in Latin America towards 1979

Population of the region	Thousands of persons	Percentage
Economically active population	75 797	100.0
Open unemployment	4 128	5.5
Equivalent unemployment through underemployment in agriculture	8 508	11.2
Equivalent unemployment through underemployment in non-agricultural sectors	8 130	10.7
Total underutilization	10 766	27.4
Total unemployed or underemployed among the active population	35 400	46.7

Source: *Diagnóstico, Políticas y Planificación del Empleo y de las Necesidades Básicas*, Santiago de Chile, ILO/PREALC, November 1978.

the percentage of total unemployed may accordingly appear low. Migration from countryside to city very often results merely in the transfer of rural underemployment to urban underemployment. In the majority of Latin American countries, between 30 and 50 per cent of the population are rural dwellers, engaged in mere subsistence activities. Because of the low nutrition levels, the inadequacy of health, education and vocational training services, and inability to save, the rural worker cannot engage in productive activities which would bring him into the market economy and enable him to improve his living conditions. This is why he moves to the city, in the illusory hope of finding work, education and prosperity.

Industrialization has not justified hopes that it would lead to more jobs, mainly because the type of technologies selected have been those that do not require much labour. In the 1950s and 1960s it was anticipated that industrialization would create work opportunities in the region on a scale large enough to reduce unemployment. However, the participation of the economically active population in the industrial sector remained virtually unchanged at almost 14 per cent over the period from 1940 to 1970, whilst the population in the urban areas increased considerably. The services sector has absorbed a large part of the unemployment originating in the rural zones, which industry could not do. This has produced an inflated tertiary sector, heavy unemployment and a marginalized population.

Contributory factors

The lack of detailed information on employment policies and prospects and the economy's relative inability to provide jobs for school-leavers have accentuated the lack of co-ordination between education and employment, mainly in the form of the extension, diversification or creation of courses—sometimes costly ones—that do not correspond to the actual needs and prospects of the labour market.

The recent increase in enrolments at all levels and in training opportunities in the region has not led to an improvement in the employment situation. There has been no reduction in the imbalances and in the quantitative and qualitative problems brought about both by the disparities between the rates of population increase and the employment rates and also by the fact that it is impossible to solve employment problems solely through education.

The employment problem has become more serious in recent years, largely due to the patterns of development adopted in many countries (production level, structure of the production system and technologies) which have an adverse effect on the demand for labour at both national and regional level. This situation could deteriorate as a result of substantial changes in the structure of the work-force in the future, the inflexibility of the education systems, which do not adapt to these changes, and the inadaptability of the production system.

In many cases, the education system is inadequately linked to the production system and fails to tap the latter's human and material resources. These resources could be used to improve the quality of the educational process and to adapt it to the realities and to the global, regional and local needs of society.

Sex appears to be an important variable in the analysis of employment problems. In some urban areas, working women generally earn less than men, or else they engage in part-time work or are underemployed; yet their level of education is generally higher than that of men in employment. The types of employment available to women may have an effect on their level of education, since many openings are in the vocational or semi-vocational category. The education levels of women in employment are higher than those of unemployed women. In many countries of the region, the highest percentage of women with jobs is to be found in the services sector, but it should be added that, within that sector, a very high proportion—women with a low level of education—are employed in domestic service.

Many firms set more store by experience than by education. Provided the workers recruited do the job with the minimum of efficiency required, employers do not replace them with others who have had a better education and training. On the other hand, some types of experience or specialized training appear to be in great demand at particular times. This suggests that preference goes to particular types of experience combined with appropriate training, rather than to absolute standards of formal education.

There is also a certain qualitative discrepancy between technical and vocational education programmes, and the needs arising from development in the formal sectors of the economy. In some cases activities for which heavy investment and high labour-absorption rates are planned are not co-ordinated with the available training opportunities. Technical and vocational education is designed more especially for young people who have already reached a certain level of education, a level beyond the reach of a large proportion of the population. This hampers their access to many of the jobs offered by industry or the services sector.

The vocational and technical education provided under the formal system is the subject of controversy and wide-ranging criticism in the region. There are those who argue that the best and only function formal education is capable of performing, and the least costly, is to offer a solid basis of general scientific and technological instruction which will subsequently enable specific skills to be developed on the job itself or through out-of-school training and apprenticeship schemes. Criticisms of the formal technical and vocational education system frequently refer to the difficulty of adapting training to technological and economic change, and it is clear that such training is not always properly related to the student's future work in industry. What is termed 'technical and vocational education' is frequently centred round a limited number of craft skills, and not always the most useful of those, or it provides training for certain tertiary activities which are of little importance.

The poor response by students in general to this educational opportunity is due to its low prestige level which in turn is due to the fact that, traditionally, it has never been a stepping-stone to higher forms of training and industry is reluctant to recognize its diplomas, which means that low salary levels and limited advancement prospects can be expected.

In most of the countries, the pupils' abilities are explored and they are given vocational guidance in the last stage of basic education or the first part of secondary education, before diversification into industrial, agricultural, commercial, teacher-training, artistic and other courses. But in many cases this is never done, and the students are channelled into the specialized subject areas at random, on the basis of questionable selection criteria. In some cases where exploratory work and vocational guidance are undertaken in the course of the curriculum, the work done has little relevance to the progress of science and practical applications of technology, which students can observe in everyday life outside school.

As a result of the growing awareness of the need for alternative ways of educating the people and preparing them for work, special attention is now being devoted to out-of-school and non-formal vocational and technical education. The programmes range from highly systematic courses such as the accelerated training schemes (SENA, SENAI, etc.) to activities organized by the armed forces, secular or religious private institutions, trade unions, academies of various kinds, and so on. There are also correspondence courses, mobile training units, rural community development programmes, agricultural extension work, community development schemes, prison workshops, courses in handicrafts, co-operative training, etc. However, in spite of the efforts made, large numbers of young people have neither been trained nor learnt their trade in a systematic way. Only a small minority in technical and vocational schools and centres have received training in the true sense of the term or theoretical instruction related to employment. A number of surveys have revealed, for example, that a high percentage of qualified craft workers learnt their trade 'on the job', and approximately two-thirds of the firms continue to train their young employees in this way. In small and medium-sized industries, the situation is similar or perhaps even worse. In 1973, according to estimates made in various countries in the region, only slightly more than 2 per cent of the work-force was catered for by institutions providing accelerated technical and vocational education.

Education in rural areas

A study of educational inequalities in the region as a whole shows that the rural population of Latin America, which represented no less then 35.6 per cent of the total population in 1980,[1] is fundamentally excluded from social progress. The educational opportunities available in rural areas fall notably short of those provided in cities. In large parts of the countries in the region only primary education is available, and even then the course is shorter than in the cities. Such circumstances make access to secondary and higher education extremely difficult for the rural population.

Geographical and economic factors account for this situation in no small measure. The enormous distances, communication difficulties, scattered settlements and villages, the system of land-ownership, with its two extremes—*latifundia* and *minifundia*—and unfair forms of land-ownership are some of these factors. According to studies carried out by ECLA, in 1975 some 1 per cent of the landowners throughout the region held more than 62 per cent of the land, while 75 per cent of the landowners held only 4.5 per cent. These are some of the factors that have a powerful effect on the situation. Moreover, education authorities in general, whether intentionally or not, in fact pay more attention to education in urban areas than in rural areas.

Schools in rural areas usually have one, two or three grades, which are taught by one teacher. It is estimated that there are over 100,000 schools of this kind in the region. In a study published by Abner Prada in connection with the project on Development and Education in Latin America and the Caribbean, sponsored jointly by Unesco, ECLA and UNDP, the educational situation in Latin American rural areas is summarized as follows.

Around 1971, over 80 per cent of the schools in Colombia, the Dominican Republic, Guatemala, Paraguay and Venezuela were one-teacher schools.

Despite the efforts made for over thirty years to introduce the complete course for all schools, it is evident that teachers continue to experience considerable difficulties in the application of multi-level teaching methods. Similarly, parents do not readily accept that one teacher alone can efficiently take a number of grades at the same time. In this respect, the system has failed to overcome the most elementary difficulties connected with teacher-training, supervision and technical assistance, and the adaptation of classrooms.

1. *Boletín demográfico de CELADE* (Santiago de Chile, Centro Latinoamericano de Demografía), Vol. XII, No. 23.

As rural enrolment statistics are incomplete, they do not give an overall picture of the region. For example, in Brazil in 1970, the enrolment ratios for the 8–12 age-group (the group with the highest proportion of enrolments) were between 91 and 98.7 per cent in urban areas but only between 46.5 and 58.6 per cent in rural areas.

The interpretation of data such as these would require an analysis of the composition of the enrolment total by grades and ages, showing figures for repetitions, over-age pupils and drop-outs. It has been established that the first-grade repetition rates in rural areas in five countries (Colombia, the Dominican Republic, Ecuador, Guatemala and Panama) range from 20.5 to 36.5 per cent; the corresponding figures for the second grade are from 17 to 25.6 per cent; and the figures for the third grade are from 12.4 to 22.5 per cent.

The drop-out rates in rural areas (for a total of eleven countries) in the second half of the 1960s were 46.9 per cent between the first and second grade and 36.3 per cent between the second and third grade. Of the pupils enrolled in the first grade, 8 per cent completed the sixth grade.

On the basis of enrolment figures of less than 50 per cent in many cases, we may say that 5 per cent of school-age children in rural areas complete their primary education; the rest do not reach this level.

The causes of absenteeism, repetition and dropping out lie both within and outside the education system. In general, greater attention is given to the study of external factors related to the socio-economic and cultural realities of rural communities, whose quality of life we have discussed earlier in this book. Such factors are: the dispersion and isolation of the rural population; the distance between home and school; the use of children for agricultural work; the financial situation of families; malnutrition; sickness; lack of parental interest; etc. But there are other factors, intrinsic to the education system, which account for the situation to a significant degree, yet are not always studied as thoroughly as they should be.

A number of these internal causes may be singled out. In order of importance, they are: (a) the widespread shortage of teachers; (b) the inadequacy and unsuitability of technical assistance and supervision; (c) the existence of schools with two or more teachers, which offer two or three grades, adopting a form of grade organization without giving the complete primary course, so that every pupil leaving such schools is statistically classified as a drop-out; (d) the adoption of schedules and timetables that frequently fail to take account of local circumstances, climatic conditions and harvest times or other periods of intensive work which call for the efforts of the entire family; and (e) a marked split between the rural community and the school. All this is a consequence of both the structure and operation of the system, and the attitudes of those responsible for directing it. Rural communities are given very little say in the way the school caters for the school-age population. Parents are occasionally consulted or informed about certain innovations or asked to contribute to the solution of a practical problem. But serious difficulties beset attempts to introduce effective participation in the planning and implementation of activities which involve the entire community in the educational process. The education authorities tend to favour a kind of mythology of school, education, educators, curricula and methods and hold out against the introduction of essential changes; they prefer a system in which teacher-training is quite unrelated to the specific problems of the rural environment. Teacher-training establishments and other training institutions located in predominantly rural areas do not produce the kind of personnel needed there. These establishments do not identify with their areas of influence. They follow the pattern adopted by institutions in the large cities, and become poor imitations of them.

Much has been done to deal with this situation by establishing institutions and services to cater more effectively for the educational needs in rural areas. Measures of this kind are being implemented by ministries of education, health and social welfare, together with other private and public bodies, in Chile, Colombia, Guyana, Mexico, Peru, Suriname and Venezuela, to quote only a few examples, by means of programmes for maternity- and child-welfare, medical aid and food, family and health education, and instruction concerning nutrition. In certain countries, the schools themselves are used as one of the main centres for these activities.

A noteworthy feature of the considerable efforts made by various countries in the region in the past decade to improve educational opportunities and standards in rural areas is the system of 'nuclear' planning; some countries have long-standing experience of this type of educational organization, while in others it has only recently been introduced. School nuclei are usually composed of several primary schools, which are generally 'incomplete' schools, known as 'satellite', 'sectional' or 'associate' schools, grouped around a basic school providing the full course, the aim being to ensure that pupils can complete the full primary or basic general course with, in some cases, emphasis on agricultural studies or pre-vocational training. Such nuclei are found, for instance, in Bolivia, Costa Rica, the Dominican Republic, Ecuador, El Salvador, Honduras, Mexico and Nicaragua.

In some countries there is a nuclear system in which school and out-of-school activities are linked, the object being to find more effective ways of using existing human and physical resources to the full, and of ensuring integration with the community. This is the case of the Multi-purpose Centres for Rural Development in Colombia, the Nuclear Planning Programme for Education in the Rural Environment in Ecuador, Guatemala's Programme of Educational Nuclei for Development, and the Communal Educational Nuclei in Peru. In countries such as Brazil, Cuba and Panama, the nuclear system operates in such a way that the network of educational facilities is composed of several primary or basic schools grouped around a complete secondary or lower-secondary school, so that they form interlinked educational units which ensure the natural progression of primary-school leavers to the secondary level and accordingly offer wider educational opportunities.

Joint programmes are being undertaken in many countries by different public and private sectors, education being a key factor in these. In some cases these are socio-economic development projects promoted by other sectors, education being allotted an important role in the achievement of the project targets. Examples are the development projects which are being undertaken by various secretariats of state at the federal level, in conjunction with the state authorities and with the aid of various Specialized Agencies of the United Nations system, in the Mexican states of Chiapas (Development Programme for the Chiapas Highlands, PRODESCH), Oaxaca (Development Programme for the Miahuatlán-Pochutla Highlands, PRODEAMP) and Quintana Roo (Development Programme for the Maya Area, PRODEMAY); the integrated rural development programmes being implemented by various ministries in conjunction with regional development corporations and with international or bilateral co-operation in areas of the Bolivian departments of Cochabamba, Chuquisaca, La Paz, Pando, Potosí and Tarija; the programmes of this kind being carried out in various rural areas in Honduras as, for example, in the Lower Aguán area; and the Integrated Rural Development Project implemented in the region of Los Lagos, in Chile (ninth region). In other cases, the education sector appears to be taking the initiative in promoting integrated rural development, as in the case of the Centres for Rural Development in Colombia, the Educational Nuclei for Development in Guatemala and the Communal Educational Nuclei in Peru.

Illiteracy

The expansion of the education system in recent decades has checked the increase in illiteracy, particularly in relative terms. However, the illiteracy situation is still causing much concern, not merely because of the very high number of illiterate adults, but on account of the data (to which reference has already been made) showing the proportion of the child population not attending school and the high drop-out rates in primary education.

Without practice in reading and writing, a school education of no more than two or three years (which is the amount of schooling received by many hundreds of thousands of children) is not sufficient to prevent a relapse into illiteracy.

According to the estimates of the Unesco Office of Statistics, 44 million out of 159 million adults (persons aged 15 and over) in Latin America and the Caribbean were illiterate in 1970. This means that the region had an illiteracy rate of 28 per cent in the year in question; in other words, just over a quarter of the adult population was illiterate.

The distribution of illiteracy varies considerably from country to country. As censuses were taken in different years in the various countries of the region over the 1960–76 period, the Office of Statistics endeavoured to standardize data relating to 1970 and projections for 1980 by grouping them on four levels according to the literacy rates achieved.

These estimates were prepared in the light of recent trends observed both in the illiteracy rates and in the enrolment ratios in the countries under review.

On the basis of this table, the situation regarding illiteracy in 1980 was as follows:

1. Rates over 40 per cent (Guatemala and Haiti).
2. Rates between 25 and 40 per cent (Bolivia, Dominican Republic, El Salvador, Honduras and Nicaragua).
3. Rates between 10 and 25 per cent (Brazil, Colombia, Ecuador, Mexico, Panama, Paraguay, Peru and Venezuela).
4. Rates below 10 per cent (Antigua, Argentina, Barbados, Chile, Costa Rica, Cuba, Grenada, Guyana, Jamaica, St Kitts-Nevis-Anguilla, St Vincent, Trinidad and Tobago, and Uruguay).

The highest illiteracy rates obviously occur among the older section of the population and inhabitants of rural areas. There is also a very high degree of correlation between poverty or destitution and illiteracy and between illiteracy and systems of land-ownership in which the *latifundio* predominates.

Illiteracy among young people continues to decrease, and the growing expansion of primary education gives grounds for hope that a considerable proportion of the children who are now reaching school age or who are already enrolled in school will not have to suffer the ill-effects of the ignorance that goes hand in hand with illiteracy. However, considerable efforts will still be needed if literacy training is to be provided for the large numbers of adults who are illiterate. In 1970, the illiteracy rate was 24.8 per cent for males aged 15 and over and 31.3 per cent for females in the same age-group. There are some countries where the rural illiteracy rate is four times higher than the urban rate. In several countries the rural illiteracy rate is over 50 per cent, and in some the rate for illiteracy among women is over 70 per cent.

Such illiteracy among large numbers of people seriously reduces their opportunities for personal development, which is primarily a matter of human dignity and the need to possess certain basic knowledge in order to make any progress in one's cultural development. Furthermore, illiteracy presents a formidable obstacle to economic development, since the efficiency of production systems increasingly calls for skilled workers; in political and social terms, illiteracy considerably restricts the effective participation of all in the rights and duties of citizenship which is so desirable.

On the occasion of International Literacy Day, in 1978, the Director-General of Unesco, Amadou-Mahtar M'Bow, drew attention to the threefold dimension of literacy, which is a moral right, an essential need and a prerequisite for the establishment of a new and more just international order:

From the ethical point of view, it is no longer permissible to leave a large part of the world's population on the periphery of the vast current of intellectual exchanges which, throughout the five continents, is leading to the intermingling of ideas, methods and techniques, mastery of which is the key to progress. Nor is it permissible today, within nations themselves, to perpetuate the political inequalities which are born of illiteracy.

The Universal Declaration of Human Rights proclaims that: 'Everyone has the right to freedom of thought, conscience and religion ... the right of education ... and the right fully to participate in the cultural life of the community.' How is it conceivable that these rights, now regarded as inalienable, can be applied in practical terms other than by every individual first grasping the alphabet of his own language? Only through learning to read does a man assume his full responsibility as a citizen. If he cannot read, he is powerless to realize the whole of his civic and political potential, neither can he exercise power at any level whatever in modern society.

It is true, of course, that in terms of practical achievement, man has always been able to live and be productive without learning to read or write. But with machinery, the implements of work become a stronger determining factor than manpower in the productive process because they incorporate more and more scientific and technological elements, and this creates insuperable obstacles for the illiterate population.

Part Three

The main lines of emphasis
of the Mexico City Conference

The Mexico City Declaration[1]

The Regional Conference of Ministers of Education and Those Responsible for Economic Planning of Member States in Latin America and the Caribbean, convened by Unesco and held in Mexico City from 4 to 13 December 1979, met in a highly encouraging spirit of consensus regarding the crucial importance of the current period of history for the countries of the region in relation to the general world situation, with clear awareness of the fact that a new stage had been reached, calling for solidarity in the affirmation of the culture unique to that part of the globe, and readiness on the part of its peoples to assume responsibility for their own destiny.

A lofty tone and a marked sense of responsibility were the key-notes of the Conference in the discussions concerning the decisive role to be assigned to education within a new style of development, that is, balanced development that would help to redirect economic activities towards greater social homogeneity and towards the production of goods and services that were genuine social and national necessities. It was therefore one of the tasks of education to give a human dimension to development by recognizing its own basic potential to build a future marked by greater cultural autonomy, greater harmony and justice in social and economic conditions, and by fulfilment of those values essential to human dignity that the peoples of the region deserved and demanded.

The Conference, having acknowledged the sustained effort that had been made by the countries of the region in the past decade to develop education, and the very noteworthy achievements in the quantitative expansion of systems and in the improvement of educational content and processes, nevertheless recognized that serious shortcomings still persisted, such as the extreme poverty of vast sectors of the population in most of the countries, and

---

1. Text of the Declaration approved by acclamation by the Regional Conference of Ministers of Education and Those Responsible for Economic Planning of Member States in Latin America and the Caribbean (Mexico City, 4-13 December 1979).

continuing low enrolment rates in some of them; the existence in the region of 45 million illiterates out of an adult population of 159 million; an unduly high drop-out rate in the early years of schooling; education systems and content that were very often ill-suited to the population for which they were intended; maladjustments in the relationship between education and work; the poor linking of education with economic, social and cultural development and in some cases faulty organization and administration of education systems, which still bore the stamp of heavy centralization from a normative and functional point of view. In the light of the foregoing, the Conference adopted the following Declaration:

The Conference declares:

That a developed nation is one whose people are well-informed, cultured, efficient, productive, responsible and possess a sense of solidarity;

That no country can extend its development beyond the stage reached by its education;

That development is measured not merely by the goods or resources that a community can command, but essentially by the quality of the individuals who produce or use them;

That *being*, not *having*, should predominate in the framing and shaping of the overall development policies of the various countries;

That education is an essential tool for the release of man's highest potential to create a more just and balanced society, and that political and economic independence cannot be fully attained unless the population is educated, has a firm grasp of reality and assumes responsibility for its destiny;

That there is an urgent need to intensify educational action as a necessary condition for the achievement of authentic development and to bring educational systems into line with the governing principles of social justice, so that they strengthen awareness, participation, solidarity and organizing ability, especially among underprivileged groups;

That the forging of adequate structural links between formal and non-formal education will make a major contribution to the achievement of development in the region;

That education should give pride of place to the transmission of moral values, the dignity of human life and the development of the individual, in a world increasingly torn by conflict and violence, against which background those values should be recognized and respected;

That the relationship between education and culture is being increasingly affected by the impact of the mass media, which have expanded very rapidly in the region and are exerting a powerful influence over the daily lives of all sectors of society, an influence which should make a positive contribution to education;

That the success that is sought in transforming curricula will depend on how such transformations interact with the specific needs, interests and problems of the social groups of the community;

That the effort entailed by the development of the region will have to assume an integrated form in such a way that education, science, technology, culture, communication, the removal of linguistic barriers, the relationship to work, social and political organization and economic progress will all tend to work towards the fundamental goal of the well-being of mankind;

That there is a need to strengthen scientific development, which, through activities of research, reflection, observation and creative experience and intuition, is conducive to the generation of new knowledge;

That uninterrupted development and progress in all fields of knowledge, and especially in science and technology, and economic and social transformations require that education systems be designed and operate within the context of life-long education, that a close relationship be established between school and out-of-school education and that appropriate use be made of the scope offered by the mass media;

That the training of people who are capable of accepting the implications of their own culture and of building scientific progress into it is essential if they are to create, develop and adapt appropriate technologies, as required by the differing contexts of the region;

That education, without prejudice to its universal scope, must essentially promote knowledge of the realities of the country, neighbouring countries and the region as objectively as possible if the past is to be retrieved, substance to be given to the present and guidelines to be laid down for the future;

That there is a need to establish a new international economic order as a basic prerequisite if the countries of the region are to carry out their national projects and consequently move on to higher levels of development that will satisfy their legitimate national needs, particularly in the fields of education, employment and productive work;

That international, intra-regional and bilateral co-operation should be instrumental in developing a renewed respect for the national goals and interests of all peoples and in ensuring that progress is made towards a new international economic order that will take account of the needs, features and aspirations of our peoples, with a view to contributing to the strengthening of co-operation among the States of the region, while fostering joint activities that will bring about greater social justice.

The Conference further declares that the Member States should:

Provide a minimum of 8 to 10 years' general education and establish as their goal to incorporate all children of school age in the system not later than 1999, in accordance with national education policies;

Adopt a clear-cut policy with a view to eradicating illiteracy before the end of the century and to extending educational services for adults;

Allocate increasingly substantial budgets to education until not less than 7 or 8 per cent of the gross national product is earmarked for educational purposes, with the aim of making up for the existing shortfall and of ensuring that education will make a full contribution to development and become the driving force behind it;

Give highest priority to providing for the least privileged population groups, who mainly live in rural and suburban areas and whose condition calls for urgent action and the provision of a variety of opportunities in keeping with their real-life situations, with the aim of surmounting the considerable differences in living conditions still existing between them and other groups;

Undertake the necessary reforms which will ensure that education takes into account the features, needs, aspirations and cultural values of every people, and which will give impetus to and renovate science teaching and will be instrumental in forging closer links between education systems and the world of work;

Use all available means, ranging from the school and the communication media to natural resources, and make a special effort to transform curricula at an early opportunity so as to make them more relevant to the needs of underprivileged groups, while relying for that purpose on the active participation of the population involved;

Adopt effective measures for renovating systems for the training of teachers, prior to, and following their qualification, in order to provide them with the possibility of adding to and updating their stock of knowledge and teaching capability;

Assist teachers in economic and social terms by creating working conditions that will ensure that they enjoy a position in keeping with their social importance and professional dignity;

Ensure, by viewing economic growth within the broader context of social development, that educational planning is closely linked to the economic, social and overall planning of each country;

Give special attention to the formulation of objectives and programmes for the quantitative expansion and qualitative improvement of higher education, reconciling university autonomy with the sovereignty of the State;

Ensure that educational planning promotes the participation and incorporation of all groups and institutions involved in one way or another in both formal and non-formal educational endeavours;

Ensure educational organization and administration in keeping with new requirements which, in most countries of the region, demand greater decentralization of decision-making and organizational processes, greater flexibility as a means of ensuring multi-sectoral action and lines of emphasis that will provide an incentive to innovation and change.

The Conference appeals:

To the Member States:

To set themselves, for the forthcoming decades, the fundamental and vitally urgent task of combating extreme poverty by using all available resources and means to ensure the general introduction of complete primary or basic education for all children of school age, to eliminate illiteracy and to intensify, gradually and thoroughly, programmes designed to make full provision for children of pre-school age who live in conditions of social deprivation;

To continue to promote the exchange of experience and co-operation with a view to facing, together, the present-day challenges of education and to devise courses of action that will lead to full development of their potentialities and the strengthening of national independence.

To all those participating in the task of education in the region:

To associate themselves with the main lines of thrust, reflections and recommendations of this Conference so that, through their day-to-day work, their experience and their critical acumen, they can contribute to the effective implementation of the objectives formulated here of broadening, speeding up and renovating the educational process in all the countries of the region.

To the international, regional and subregional organizations:

To make available all their technical, administrative and financial capacity to the Governments of the region for the purpose of giving support to their policies and programmes in the field of education.

To Unesco:

To continue to collaborate assiduously in the rapid establishment of a new international economic order;

To take the initiative of putting forward a major project embodying the fundamental features of this Declaration;

To publicize this Mexico Declaration by all possible means.

The Conference expresses, lastly, its deepest gratitude:

To Unesco, for having convened this vitally important Conference and for having endeavoured to ensure that it effectively fulfilled its purpose of working for the further development of the education systems of the countries of Latin America and the Caribbean and accordingly of promoting the progress and well-being of its peoples;

To the Government and People of Mexico, for their warm hospitality and their fraternal welcome, and for having provided the most appropriate conditions and facilities for ensuring that this appointment with history would take place under the most propitious circumstances.

Mexico City, 13 December 1979.

The concept of development: the role of education and science

In his opening address, the President of the Mexico City Conference, Mr Solana, the Minister of Education of Mexico, referred to the concept of development in the following terms:

In the long history of development thinking, we have already rejected development models that are not consistent with our experience or the genuine aspirations of our peoples. We cannot look upon development as the repeated imitation of stages which other countries have gone through before us, or merely as economic growth or, again, exclusively as the boosting of efficiency and technology.

Since the Conference held in Santiago in 1962, our choice has been development that will, at one and the same time, be economic, social and cultural and we have embodied in our objectives more wide-ranging processes side by side with those of an economic kind. But even a definition such as this is imperfect. It does not highlight the end-purpose of development which is man himself, in his dignity as an individual and his responsibility as a member of society.

In the last resort, development involves people. If we lose sight of that fact, we run the risk of becoming countries that may be prosperous and even powerful but will hardly be developed, after the manner of a number of oil-exporting countries which have come into wealth but have not defeated underdevelopment.

Goods do not confer quality on life unless a change takes place in the people who produce and use them. Technology does not improve life if the people handling it do not control their own destinies. Power does not bring about the improvement of peoples if it is not exercised as a service rendered. The key factor is human betterment. It is *being*, not *having*.

This is a concept of development which embraces all aspects of the life of a society, integrating them in a consistent collective project to the extent that they are consonant with moral and cultural aims (and, of course, economic aims), having their roots in the people's historical heritage and commanding broad allegiance among its members.

The Director-General of Unesco put this clearly in an address to the Governing Council of UNDP in June 1979, when he said:

Such a concept of development cannot be put into practice without the full flowering of the latent potential of each society, particularly in its socio-cultural dimensions, namely, culture, education, science and communication.

To say that any development activity which underestimates these dimensions necessarily leads to increasingly serious social, material and moral imbalances, does not, however, mean that a universal model exists for their harmonious integration into the process of economic growth. On the contrary, it suggests that there are several paths leading to this goal.

The fact is that multidimensional endogenous development cannot be the same everywhere, since it presupposes by definition some way of grafting it on to different societies, each with their original cultures and traditions. The most tragic error to date has been to believe that it was desirable, and possible, to replace genuine cultures— frequently dismissed as anachronistic—by others considered to be more suited to the modern world.

We now know that all cultures have a capacity for change and progress as well as a capacity for inertia; and that it is for every society to make the choices necessary to enable the former to develop at the expense of the latter. Here is where we find the invariable specificity of the ways and styles of development peculiar to each society. Here, too, in short, the key to their economic vitality is to be found.

Today, each developing country wishes to tap its own resources and is at the same time seeking a fairer distribution of wealth at national and international level. This does not, of course, rule out the transfer of know-how. Nevertheless, respect for cultural identity demands that the activities of the foreign countries engaged in the transfer of know-how coexist with the emergence of original styles of development, avoiding any form of cultural domination based on scientific and technological power. This approach calls for a revision of some of the current thinking on international aid, upon which we shall comment later in this book.

With regard to Latin America, ECLA described this integral, organic approach in its Appraisals of the Implementation of the International Development Strategy in the 1970s as follows:

Development should be conceived of as an integral process characterized by the achievement of economic and social targets which ensure the effective participation of the population in the development process and in its benefits. To this end it is essential to make far-reaching structural changes in this field as a prerequisite for the process of integral development which it is sought to achieve.

[It therefore stressed that] economic growth is a necessary but not by itself a sufficient condition to ensure full social and human development. This requires the introduction of institutional reforms and appropriate policies within the framework of an integral and organic conception of the development process. The results of this economic growth must be more fairly distributed so that, in addition to ensuring the active participation of the different sectors of society, it will also be possible to create juster societies where human beings will find better possibilities for the fullest development of their potential. [For this,] it will be necessary to introduce the reforms required to guarantee the access of the population to employment, education, health and other social, public and private services.

In the same appraisal, it was noted that:

Most of the burden of the measures and strategies for economic recovery frequently falls on the poorest and most helpless strata of the population, in the form of a marked reduction in public spending on education, health and other social services for the people.

It was likewise established that:

This experience has given rise to some scepticism with regard to the traditional beliefs that economic growth would of itself bring with it the solution to the serious and widespread problems of poverty, uneven income distribution, and unemployment and underemployment, which have existed and continue to do so despite the considerable development of the forces of production, [for] the fruits of economic growth have not been fairly distributed among the different population groups. Indeed, if present conditions continue, it can be foreseen with a high degree of certainty that the share of the poorer strata in the fruits of future growth will tend to remain at completely inadequate levels.

In its discussions, the Mexico City Conference confirmed earlier assessments of the limitations, inconsistencies and structural faults to be observed in the development of the countries of the region, and, in particular, the failure of economic growth to permeate all strata of society. It was pointed out that mere economic growth did not necessarily lead to well-being, and that wealth, important as it was, did not always guarantee development. Attention was drawn to the fact that 40 per cent of the population of the region were living in critical poverty. The predominant development model in certain cases was seen as one of dependence on foreign markets and capital, accompanied by forms of internal colonialism penalizing certain areas, which were condemned to ever-greater social exclusion, and also certain population groups for whom, owing to the lack of equitable income distribution policies, average economic growth was totally meaningless as far as their own living standards were concerned.

The concentration of vast wealth on the one hand, and, on the other, of tremendous enduring poverty was dividing certain societies into two camps, with the attendant and considerable danger of a violent disruption of peace, and of the most needy sectors of the population seeing their chances of living in dignity still further reduced; all this, moreover, was happening in a continent richly endowed with natural resources.

Mention was also made of the severe cultural alienation affecting certain societies, the damage caused by the absorption—accelerated in some cases by the action of the mass media—of patterns of conduct based on the accumulation of wealth and consumer goods, the emergence of artificial needs that only the most privileged could satisfy, and the low status accorded to the distinctive cultural features of various population groups in the region.

These considerations led the conference to stress the need for a new conception of development and of policies to promote it, which should focus on the social need to involve all sectors of the population in the development effort and in the distribution of its benefits, in keeping with a comprehensive approach combining economic, social and cultural goals. It was also agreed that there was a need to remedy the virtual 'exhaustion' of certain life-styles and that development should be aimed essentially at providing for human needs by means of a process of liberation enabling all men and women to make full use of their capacities. In certain cases, far-reaching structural changes would be necessary to enable the whole population to gain access to the benefits of economic growth: employment, education and other social and cultural services.

Attention was also drawn to the importance of the moral and human values that should inspire this new type of development, which had to reconcile the cultural identity of each nation with the requirements of economic growth and modernization, and national interests with those of other countries, so that more equitable relationships might be established between them. In the world context, this new approach to development found expression in the concept of a new international economic order. Moreover, current conditions in Latin America and the Caribbean, and the area's natural wealth, made the necessary changes perfectly feasible in this region.

A humanist approach to development

The humanist concept of development specifies certain aims for the development process, the first of which is that it should be beneficial to man. This implies that the distribution of the benefits obtained through economic improvement and, similarly, the distribution of the efforts and sacrifices involved, should be governed by the principle of fairness and social justice. Second, it should bear upon all the dimensions of human life: it should be aimed, not merely at raising people's living standards, but at their spiritual, material, personal and social advancement.

This has, in fact, been a leitmotif of the various conferences of ministers. At the first of the conferences held to consider the link between education and economic development (Santiago, 1962), one illustrious participant, Torres Bodet, Minister of Education and Head of the Mexican delegation at that meeting, made the following statement:

We do not believe that we have to create material wealth and nothing else; we have to make people culturally aware and educate them for life in a free society. Of course, we have to invest in the expansion of the educational services in order to speed up the implementation of economic and social programmes in all our countries. But progress must enable us to bring greater effectiveness to the performance of our duties as peoples whose aspiration is not so much to produce in order to be rich as to ensure a more consistent form of independence and to contribute in a more constructive way to peace and the advancement of mankind.

Such views were not untimely in a period when certain sectors saw the relationship between education and development in predominantly utilitarian terms, implying that education was subordinate to the needs and demands of the economy. Furthermore, the idea of development has frequently been associated with an essentially materialistic outlook characterized by the increased production of goods and greater affluence. Alexis Carrel addressed himself to this question in his widely read work, *Man, the Unknown*,[1] in which

1. Alexis Carrel, *Man, the Unknown*, New York/London, Harper & Brothers, 1935.

he gave an all too accurate description of the grim consequences of the way development was being interpreted. He wrote:

Modern industry is based on the conception of the maximum production at lowest cost, in order that an individual or group of individuals may earn as much money as possible. It has expanded without any idea of the true nature of the human beings who run the machines, and without giving any consideration to the effects produced on the individuals and on their descendants by the artificial mode of existence imposed by the factory. The great cities have been built with no regard for us. The shape and dimensions of the skyscrapers depend entirely on the necessity of obtaining the maximum income per square foot of ground, and of offering to the tenants offices and apartments that please them. This caused the construction of gigantic buildings where too large masses of human beings are crowded together. Civilized men like such a way of living. While they enjoy the comfort and banal luxury of their dwelling, they do not realize that they are deprived of the necessities of life. The modern city consists of monstrous edifices, of cars, and of dark, narrow streets full of gasoline fumes, coal dust, and toxic gases, torn by the noise of the taxicabs, trucks and trolleys, and thronged ceaselessly by great crowds. Obviously, it has not been planned for the good of its inhabitants.

Far from abating, the situation against which Carrel inveighed over fifty years ago has become more widespread. It represents one of the most important reasons for modern man's frustration and malaise, and is reflected in psychological and moral disturbances and the powerful ferment of social unrest. This raises the eminently contemporary question of the 'quality of life', that is to say, the overriding need to seek an improvement in the conditions of man's material, physical, mental and spiritual existence. In short, in the words of one speaker at the Mexico City Conference, 'the end-purpose of development is man himself, in his dignity as an individual and his responsibility as a member of society. . . . Goods do not confer quality on life unless a change takes place in the people who produce and use them.'

The role of education

The founders of the Latin American nations clearly grasped the fundamental nature of the role played by education in the life and development of societies. At the present time, as the Mexico City Declaration points out, 'no country can extend its development beyond the stage reached by its education'. Education thus forms the very backbone of development.

After consideration of the educational situation in the region, the conclusion was reached that an education characterized by substantial dropping out in the early years of primary education and the consequent creation of millions of illiterates, by disparities between the instruction provided and the type of employment available, which inevitably leads to frustration, and by the transmission of cultural models that reflected minority interests, was an education that aggravated injustices and imbalances, and helped to create uncertainty and social conflict, thereby quickening the erosion of national identity. If education was to make an effective contribution to development, it had to foster the creative potential of the pupils and develop their scientific and technical skills in order to further their own advancement and that of their countries. One of the main features of a developed society is the high level of efficiency of the functional units, namely the economic, political, educational, scientific and technical units, which are essential aspects of that society. Such efficiency depends primarily on the level and quality of the training of the people who carry out these activities.

In development, as seen from this new angle, education is called upon to play a crucial role, releasing the creative potential of millions of men and women to further their own advancement and that of their countries, and developing knowledge, attitudes, civic and moral patterns of conduct and scientific and technical skills that will foster such development. If education is to fulfil this role effectively, far-reaching revision and realignment of its objectives, content and methods are required, as well as modification of the internal and external factors and elements that govern its efficiency.

It would then have to meet a number of requirements in that it would have to satisfy the demand for the many professionals needed by society and at the same time serve as a mechanism of social change, providing for universal instruction and the advancement of those who are most capable of pursuing their studies. This approach imposes a new task on education in the sense that it should, at all levels, serve to stimulate the inevitable advance of science and technology.

The role of science

'Knowledge is power', said Francis Bacon. We live in a society dominated by science and technology. In view of the impact of these activities on development processes, it is of fundamental importance that scientific progress be directed towards the good of man and society.

In his work, *Scientific Outlook*,[1] Bertrand Russell referred to the influence of scientific progress on modern life in the following words:

Art was already well developed before the last glacial epoch, as we know from the admirable pictures in caves; of the antiquity of religion we cannot speak with equal confidence, but it is highly probable that it is coeval with art. At a guess one might suppose that both have existed for some eighty thousand years. Science as an important force begins with Galileo, and has therefore existed for some three hundred years. During the first half of that short period it remained a pursuit of the learned, which did not affect the thoughts or habits of ordinary men. It is only during the last hundred and fifty years that science has become an important factor in determining the everyday life of everyday people. In that short time it has caused greater changes than had occurred since the days of the ancient Egyptians. One hundred and fifty years of science have proved more explosive than five thousand years of pre-scientific culture.

Considering these themes in the Latin American context, the conference pointed out that national independence, cultural as well as economic, and the

1. Bertrand Russell, *Scientific Outlook*, London, George Allen & Unwin, 1931.

elimination of external dependencies required greater efforts to develop scientific and technical research and training. It was generally agreed that this should include the social and human sciences, which must be brought to bear on the definition of goals and objectives if development was to have a 'human face'. In this connection, the gradual disappearance of social scientists and of social science training centres from many Latin American universities and countries was seen as a serious problem.

Scientific and technical development may indeed be considered inadequate in many countries of the region. Scientific and technological research is not given its proper place and plays scarcely any part in the training of graduates, who have little contact with scientists in their formative years. In some countries of the region, the importance of scientific research in higher education, far from being increased, has been reduced, and a growing proportion of research is conducted in the private sector or in non-university institutions of the public sector.

This trend should be reversed for many reasons, including the value of research as a means of ensuring the high quality of education. There is, however, the acute problem of the limited resources available to universities in both human and financial terms. Academic staff largely absorbed by teaching duties should be enabled to give a reasonable proportion of their time to research, and researchers should also devote some of their time to teaching at the higher level, as is the custom in certain countries. Students and young scientists showing the inclination and aptitude for research should be identified and given proper incentive and encouragement.

Although the role of fundamental research remains essential, greater attention should be given to applied research for the solution of specific problems. This requires an interdisciplinary approach, co-operation with the productive sector and different groups in the community and a close relationship between research and development goals. Research undertaken by institutions of higher education should be related to national policies and be an integral part of national plans for research in the service of development. The research undertaken would then no longer reflect merely personal interests but would correspond to national requirements.

The Director-General of Unesco, Amadou-Mahtar M'Bow, summed up the importance of the contribution of science and technology to development, as well as the salient features of the present situation, in the following manner, in an address given to the Preparatory Committee for the New International Development Strategy, on 20 June 1979:

The establishment of a scientific and technological basis in a country should serve to promote a more autonomous form of development and safeguard its cultural identity and its sovereignty. That is why we must base our approach on the fact that each culture possesses an endogenous potential, an aptitude of its own for scientific and technological progress, and that it is that aptitude that must be developed and enhanced. No one would suggest that each nation should independently repeat the discoveries made by all the others: but in drawing on the universal bank of acquired scientific knowledge, which is the common property of mankind, it should strive to assimilate knowledge with the aim of finding original solutions to its own problems.

If we are to base progress on endogenous scientific and technological development, however, there is an urgent need to create in each country a national scientific potential, starting with the establishment of the necessary infrastructures and the training of a sufficiently large and competent scientific community. It is here that international co-operation is most badly needed—and here that, by and large, it is lacking. Let us look at a few figures in this connection.

The total number of scientists and engineers engaged in research and experimental development throughout the world (with the exception of China and a few other countries for which figures are not available) was estimated to be about 2.8 million in 1974, halfway through the Second Development Decade. Of these, 2.6 million—i.e. 94 per cent—were working in the developed countries.

In those countries, therefore, there were some 2,600 scientists and research workers per million inhabitants—as against about 100 in the so-called developing countries: 77 in Africa, 179 in Latin America and 355 in Asia, including Japan.

Expenditure on research and experimental development throughout the world in 1974 (with the exception of China) came to $102,000 million, $99,000 million of which, or 97 per cent of the total, was accounted for by the developed countries, as against 3 per cent by the so-called developing countries, with $100 million, i.e. one-thousandth of the total amount, by the poorest among them.

The proportion of the gross national product spent on research and development was 2.3 per cent on average in the developed countries and 0.33 per cent in the others.

There can be no valid co-operation until such imbalances are courageously and radically righted.

New education policies

Just over a century ago, Friedrich Nietzsche wrote: 'The day will come when politics will be concerned solely with educational problems.'

Needless to say, this prediction has not yet come true. On the other hand, there is no denying that education is bound up with a variety of exceedingly important political problems, since it has to meet an incessant flow of new requirements in connection, *inter alia*, with the decolonization and political independence of numerous countries, the access of the broad masses to education, industrialization, urbanization, the increased tempo of history and the expansion of the mass media.

This gives an indication of the limited scope of the traditional systems for meeting such requirements at a pace which matches or even approaches that of rising social, political and economic expectations. It is therefore necessary to cease thinking of and administering education as if its importance were confined to the classroom.

It is interesting to note, in this respect, the situation to which Daniel Morales Gómez refers[1] when he considers the limitations under which, according to Carnoy and Levin, educators have been labouring:

Educational decisions have been made by politicians and techno- or bureaucrats and not by educators. Educators have had to take second or third place in the instigation of educational change; they have had little time, little initiative and few opportunities to step outside the classroom to see what is going on in society. Furthermore, those educators who, by training or preference, have been in a position to take part in studies, research projects or educational change processes have confined themselves, almost exclusively, to socially irrelevant information of interest to a small circle of initiates. They have treated the school as if it were independent of the social system, taking the line that their main task is to quantify, by means of significant indicators, the history of education, students, teachers, investments and results, without taking into account what is going on outside the school, why education is proceeding in one direction or

1. Daniel A. Morales Gómez (comp.), *Educación y desarrollo dependiente en América Latina*, Mexico City, Ediciones Gernika, 1979.

another or, lastly, the social value of the instruments which they are applying in their analysis. They have indulged in statistical games without looking beyond the four walls of the classroom or of their research centres; they are unaware that societies are founded on a complex network of mechanisms and economic functions, and particular forms of relationship which take on the nature of their underlying principles.

The time has come for education to be conceived as a genuinely political undertaking, mobilizing all institutional resources, whose encouragement of cultural activity would create the climate that would foster government action, while the family, trade unions, labour and youth organizations, political parties, the mass media and business would be associated with it, each in its own style and manner, yet inspired by the common aim to develop each individual's positive qualities. Thus, action to promote education will undoubtedly become a more significant basis of support for efforts to overcome underdevelopment and social exclusion.

At the Mexico City Conference, various guidelines were set out for the shaping of education policies. The first was to develop, among broad sectors of the population, an awareness of their place in history and in the world, of their power over nature and of the possible impact of their action on society. The second concerned participation based on common values and goals, overriding selfish individualism; these shared goals will undoubtedly include the preservation of cultural identity and the strengthening of national identity in the face of attempted foreign domination. Such participation implies a feeling of solidarity reflected in shared interests and values—particularly social solidarity—which will lead to a more just and fairer society. This calls for a capacity for organization, perseverance, hard work and the rational use of the means required to attain these aims and, lastly, an education concerned with occupational performance and productivity, providing an efficient training for work and also producing men and women who have a critical, responsible and creative approach to life. Seen from this angle, education policy is not merely the art of the possible, as it is customarily described. It is also the art of opening up new possibilities.

The development of such broad-ranging education policies involving requirements of this nature calls for some stimulation of education planning processes, realigning them to meet the new challenges faced by education systems today, and remedying the inadequacies of the past. The conference attached particular importance to the special role of education planning as an integral part of economic, social and cultural development planning, and to the functions it performs in regard to the expansion and democratization of education and to the improvement of its relevance and quality and its internal and external efficiency. It considered that today, more than ever before, the region has to place much greater emphasis on the principles underlying planning, such as the need to ensure that decision-making and action are consistent, to relate educational content and growth to the requirements of national development, and to make the best possible use of the resources available for education. Stress was also laid on the role which planning has to play in dealing with the serious problem of the unequal educational opportunities offered to different age-groups, social and ethnic groups, regions, areas and localities. It will be necessary to continue or expand the decentralization and regionalization of educational administration, the planning of education systems in which all sectors participate, and the training and in-service training of the technical and administrative personnel which these new activities will require.

This approach means that planning cannot be left solely to a single department or group of technicians whose special function it is. Planning should rather be conceived and conducted as a dynamic and co-ordinative social process with the participation of all the sectors involved in education both inside and outside ministries of education. Only in this way will education policies, plans and reforms become truly national and all-embracing in nature, reflect the needs and aspirations of the various regions, localities and social groups, and be adopted in a spirit of consensus which will guarantee their implementation. Of great importance in this connection is action by ministries of education to achieve better co-ordination between their own planning systems and those of the national and regional bodies for overall development planning, of the other ministries, and of autonomous public or private universities and institutions providing education.

Planning should bring together the different forms and patterns of participation. The assignment of this role to planning is both justified and demanded by the vast complexity of a modern educational system, with its ramifications and repercussions on different sectors and aspects of society. Only the active participation of the sectors concerned can lead to effective, development-geared planning. Moreover, in view of the adverse circumstances of majority groups of the population in rural areas and in the poverty-belts round the cities, planning will have to involve out-of-school education and be co-ordinated with formal education systems without neglecting its overall task of forecasting and programming educational development at national level.

One of the difficulties facing planners, which illustrates the need for planning in so far as it establishes priorities and limitations, is the inadequacy of the resources earmarked for education. The effectiveness of planning and its methods will depend to a large extent on its contribution to rationalization and the better distribution and use of the resources available, and also to efforts to discover new ways of organizing the educational process and alternative technologies that will help to overcome the problem of limited resources and of the increasing demand for education, bearing in mind that certain minimum education standards must be maintained.

Priorities in education policies

The 1980s and the target year 2000 formed the chronological frames of reference within which the conference sought to specify and define the objectives and priorities towards which education policies for the region should be directed. Various recommendations set out the line of approach to be followed in relation to broad questions of particular importance in the Latin American context such as the right to education or 'education for all', equality of opportunity and special attention for the least-privileged sectors, the quality of education and the renewal of educational administration. Other recommendations refer to problems that are closely linked to the economic and cultural development of Latin America and the Caribbean, such as: (a) education and the world of work; (b) education and rural development; (c) education and the least-privileged groups in urban areas; (d) the linking of formal and non-formal education in the context of the democratization of education and lifelong education; and (e) the responsibilities of higher education *vis-à-vis* the requirements of development and the democratization of education. With the aim of attaining such aspirations and objectives and with a view to subregional integration and the new international economic order, new forms of subregional, regional and international co-operation are being devised. This broad spectrum of goals for education policy is covered and summarized in the Mexico City Declaration, which could be regarded as a charter setting out the major principles underlying the action to be taken and the objectives to be achieved.

The right to education and equality of opportunity

In the first of its recommendations, the conference began, quite appropriately, by stating the principle of the right to education and strongly urged the Member States of the region to:

make a specific endeavour to bring about full and effective exercise of the right to education and to ensure that all children receive education of the requisite duration and quality so that illiteracy may be eradicated before the end of the present century and favourable conditions created for providing all with manifold opportunities and forms of education that will have regard for the dynamic changes taking place in the societies of the region.

The objectives of 'education for all', the democratization of education and the quality of education are still very far from becoming a reality. The vast scale of the undertaking involved is indicated by some of the figures in an earlier section: 45 million illiterate adults (28 per cent) and 11 million children between the ages of 6 and 11 who do not attend school (20 per cent).

It was recognized that this situation could not be remedied unless current trends were reversed. At present, large sectors of the population are deprived of educational facilities and as, unlike better-educated groups who are aware of the importance of such facilities, they lack the means of organization and mobilization, their illiteracy is perpetuated.

It is unrealistic to expect economic growth automatically to lead to the general extension of education or to hope that the mere expansion of current educational services will be sufficient to eliminate such high illiteracy rates. A special effort is required, within the framework of a policy specifically designed to bring about the true democratization of education. In the first place, this effort should be made outside the school and education system; it should be an effort made by society as a whole, guided by a new blueprint for social justice, human solidarity and development. Certain current development models could quite well be perpetuated—and indeed made to flourish—by dint of applying increasingly more advanced technologies, without being affected in the slightest by the existence of a growing number of illiterates. The alternative should therefore be a resolute political determination that will, in the interests of equity and true development, put an end to inequalities in the distribution of information, knowledge and culture.

In short, the democratization of education must be made a reality rather than a principle to which lip-service must be paid.

In an analysis of this question, Semia Tanguiane,[1] the Assistant Director-General for Education at Unesco, set out the prerequisites for an effective democratization of education. He pointed out, in this respect, that although equal access to education is one of the main requirements, democratization amounts to something more than equal access. It cannot be equated with the passing of formal legislation enshrining the right of access to education, nor is it merely a matter of extending the opportunities available. Democratization does not simply mean access to a certain level or form of education; the right of access to education should be extended to all and offer everyone the opportunity to continue and complete his or her education. This calls for a combination of social and educational measures (grants, provision of free

---

1. S. Tanguiane, 'Education and the Problem of its Democratization', *Prospects: Quarterly Review of Education* (Paris, Unesco), Vol. 7, No. 1, 1977, pp. 14–31.

meals, textbooks, transport, etc.) designed to help those social groups most in need of them.

It is a matter, then, of broadening the concept of the right to education on three different fronts. First, this concept is equated with equal access to education; second, it also implies that everyone should be given an equal opportunity to complete their education successfully; and, finally, it concerns the educational needs of the individual throughout his life. In the past, the knowledge (general and vocational) which a person acquired in his youth more or less sufficed for the whole of his life. Today, however, the requirements of scientific and technological progress, and the accelerated rate of social change, mean that the education received in childhood and adolescence within the formal education system can be regarded only as a basis which must be periodically built upon through other educational activities. The old concept of the right to education, which envisaged virtually nothing more than basic education, has thus been extended to cover general, vocational and lifelong education.

These new approaches to the democratization of education and equality of opportunity entail a number of requirements. Two of these requirements are of fundamental importance: first, the realignment of education systems so that rising generations will not suffer the consequences of inequality of educational opportunity; and, second, an effort to lessen the difficulties encountered by adults, and particularly by illiterate adults.

In our examination of the inequalities of educational opportunity in the section on the major issues confronting education in Latin America, attention was drawn, among other factors, to the cultural 'handicap' of children from extremely poor families and communities. In such circumstances, poor nutrition, the limited vocabulary they hear or use, and the cultural world of their home do not assist efforts to teach them. Moreover, there is frequently a conflict between two culture and value systems, and even between the languages used in the family environment and at school.

In such circumstances, the extremely important role played by families in totally different environments cannot be performed effectively. This state of affairs highlights the importance of 'parents' education', which is still at an early stage in those countries of the region where it has been introduced. As has been previously mentioned, pre-school education can play a compensatory role in this respect; unfortunately, it is most noticeably absent where it is most needed—in rural areas and in the outlying districts of large cities.

Furthermore, the structure of an education system should be flexible enough for its activities to take into account the social environment in which it operates. It should be flexible in its curricula, its methods, its calendars and timetables, its promotion systems and its schemes for drop-outs. Naturally, high priority should be given to planning the extension of the school network and other education establishments so as to cover the whole area.

Education always has to take into account the great diversity of individual abilities and aptitudes. When dealing with children from underprivileged social backgrounds, it is all the more necessary to use imagination and not be bound by set patterns, in an effort to get the most out of each child and overcome the handicap of his social environment.

The teacher's role in this work is vital. Trainee teachers should therefore be given a basic training—if only on a limited scale—which will enable them to take stock of the different factors in the social environment and study their influence on educational processes. In addition to this, teachers working in such environments will have to extend their activities outside the school premises and act as cultural extension workers in the community.

Literacy and adult education

A special approach is required to cater for those persons who did not have the opportunity to attend educational institutions during their childhood and adolescence. The major need is to provide literacy training, which the conference considered should be one of its priorities, establishing the year 2000 as the date by which the expansion of primary education and literacy campaigns should have eradicated illiteracy.

Lessons have been learnt from various campaigns and pilot projects implemented both in Latin America and the Caribbean and in other regions that will help to achieve greater efficiency in adult literacy training in future. In this context, it is important to consider the results of the Experimental World Literacy Programme (EWLP) implemented by Unesco between 1966 and 1973, with the co-operation of UNDP and other United Nations agencies in twenty countries. This programme was evaluated according to a set of rigorous methodological criteria and in an open and critical spirit. Among the many conclusions to be drawn from the programme the following may be singled out: (a) literacy work must be associated with concerted development action which will include, besides economic growth, a number of far-reaching social changes; (b) the 'uses' of literacy must therefore be viewed in the widest sense—cultural, social and political as much as vocational and economic; and (c) the nature of and procedures for international assistance for literacy action must be defined on the basis of national priorities and approaches, which implies a variety of approaches and strategies for international co-operation in this area.

The Unesco publication *Thinking Ahead*[1] looks at the question in this way: 'Literacy action is but one stage in the educational process and literacy has no purpose until it leads to further activities and the fulfilment of potential along one or other of the numerous lines connoted by the principles of lifelong education.' Literacy action should be planned and conducted in full awareness of socio-economic, cultural and ethical dimensions, the latter being rooted in the right to education.

Literacy programmes must be adapted to local conditions; each country

1. *Thinking Ahead: Unesco and the Challenges of Today and Tomorrow*, Paris, Unesco, 1977. (This work is based on Unesco's Medium Term Plan for 1977–1982.)

must define its own literacy policy on the basis of the specific problems with which it has to deal. A great variety of literacy experiments have been carried out in Latin America. In recent years, literacy work has been seen as a permanent, active form of social mobilization, and youth volunteers have been given key roles in the implementation of plans involving the combined efforts of national authorities, planners and technicians working closely with the representative sectors of the community. Examples of such campaigns are those conducted by the *Misiones Culturales* in Mexico (in the Vasconcelos period), the Cuban campaign (from 1959 onwards) and the campaign currently being conducted in Nicaragua (since March 1980). The objectives of the last-mentioned campaign were stated at the Mexico City Conference. They may be formulated as follows:

To eradicate illiteracy from Nicaragua once and for all.
To incorporate the broad masses of the population, through political and ideological 'conscientization', in the process of national reconstruction and development.
To give an impetus to the all-round development of the new Nicaraguan society, eliminating, through the 'culturalization' of the people, the causes and the adverse consequences of illiteracy, in a close relationship with the objectives set out in the sectoral and overall plans envisaged in the economic and social programme of the government of national reconstruction.
The establishment of a link with the far-reaching process of Agrarian Reform, which has turned over to the people more than half the arable land in the country.
This Campaign is intended to be permanent, in that it is not restricted to this initial stage, but will be accompanied by 'education-for-freedom' programmes for adults and followed up by post-literacy action.

Lifelong education and adult education

The idea of lifelong education has been widely discussed and put into practice in recent years. It meets a number of contemporary requirements. It provides adults with educational opportunities that were not available when they were younger. It meets the need for refresher training imposed by the rapid development of knowledge. It facilitates occupational retraining and promotion and enables the individual to lead a richer cultural life. All this calls for a re-thinking of education systems and is bringing about significant changes in education structures, and in content and teaching methods. At the same time, it fosters the participation of business concerns in education and stimulates the educational community by giving education a practical slant.

Adult education has a vitally important part to play within the framework of lifelong education. In the discussions of the International Conference on Adult Education held in Tokyo (1972), adult education was described as: (a) a means of acquiring a clear understanding, and an instrument of socialization and radical social change; (b) enabling the whole man (man at work and at leisure, the member of society and the member of a family) to attain personal fulfilment, by contributing to the development of his physical, moral and intellectual attributes; (c) preparing man to engage in productive activity and participate in the management of affairs; and (d) a means of combating economic and cultural alienation and preparing the way for the emergence of a genuinely national, liberating culture.

Most Latin Americans have not completed their education and face an alarming unemployment situation, which calls for new qualifications. In such circumstances the need to devote special attention to adult education is clear. In a reference to employment problems, mention has already been made of various vocational training activities carried out by Latin American countries. The United Nations agencies could make an extremely effective contribution to the attainment of these goals in the field of adult education. There is ILO, with its world employment programme; the Food and Agriculture Organization (FAO), for agricultural extension work, nutrition and co-operative schemes; and the World Health Organization (WHO), for health education. For its part, Unesco helps to establish organizational guidelines, structures and content specifications which will make it possible to meet the broad range of changing needs in adult education and technical education.

The quality of education

In one of its recommendations, the Mexico City Conference stated that the improvement of education is not merely a pre-condition if minimum educational standards are to be met for the entire school population, but will also be decisive in instilling in students a desire to learn and to continue their training for their working life. It therefore urged that the Member States and Unesco embark upon strenuous action to improve the quality of education, directed towards support for educational research and the provision of initial and further training for teachers and administrators, which it regarded as essential for the achievement of this objective.

The nature and the varied range of problems (which have already been described) confronting education in the Latin American and Caribbean region, as well as the high drop-out and repetition rates in schools in the region (also considered in earlier chapters) have made the quality of education a subject of great concern and interest. Today, the question of quality is one of the key issues in all education systems. While it may be that too much is expected from education, it is also evident that, in a good many cases, the deployment of vast reserves of manpower and material resources has failed to produce the desired results. None the less, it should be borne in mind that in recent years greater efforts have been made to expand the different levels of education and that their inordinate growth has necessitated a good many makeshift arrangements. It is now understood that, if the newly extended activities of educational institutions are to be efficient and effective, the quality of education must be improved.

Dr Dengo de Vargas, the Minister of Education of Costa Rica, expressed this concern for the quality of education—a concern shared by other delegations—in her report to the conference, setting out the requisite lines of action in the following terms:

At this juncture in the educational development of the country, characterized by the general extension of the educational system throughout the national territory at all levels, including the university level, with an enrolment ratio of 94 per cent in the first phase of basic general education, and intensive activity by the Instituto Nacional de Aprendizaje (INA), the improvement of the quality and efficiency of the educational processes has become the number-one task, one which is, in any case, imposed by the advance of knowledge, economic and cultural development and the impact of the mass media. This improvement is one of the declared aims of the present administration under the Ministry of Education. It entails curricular revision at the different levels of education, the formulation of new policies for the initial training, in-service training and further training of teachers, and a thorough review of the functions of advisers, inspectors, information services and educational resource services, since opportunities for improving the quality of education basically arise in the classroom. None the less, one fundamental aspect has to be reconsidered in the light of all the different influences at work in today's world. It concerns the educator's new roles in relation to society and in his dealings with the student who, as a human being, is both the end and the focal point of every educational process. The student is seen free within the educational process, as a responsible, critical and creative being existing in his own right, capable of great achievements in individual and social terms and in terms of his incorporation into the world of work. This calls for the development of new values and attitudes in the educator and in the educational institution, in view of the functions of knowledge and the dynamics of the teaching and learning process.

The concept of quality

One cannot expect the quality of education to be understood by everyone in quite the same way, as not all education systems have the same aims. None the less, there seems to be a fairly broad consensus on the conditions or requirements for good quality education. First, general education should be directed towards the fundamental, all-round development of the individual. The old treatises on education used to advocate what is today known as the development of the 'whole' man. It was customary to speak of intellectual training as a means of making man more capable of attaining truth. A fundamental function of institutions of education is to impart learning and broaden the scope of knowledge, which some see in terms of the development or release of mental abilities. Others define educational objectives in terms of their basic components and refer to humanistic, scientific and technical objectives. Any education worthy of the name must mould all these aspects into a balanced whole.

This intellectual training should go hand in hand with a training for life designed to give the individual a capacity for learning that will enable him to face the challenges of a constantly changing technological world; an aesthetic education that will help him to discover beauty and, more important, his own ability to create beauty; and, lastly, by developing both the individual and social dimensions of the personality, a moral education which, for many people, is linked to a religious, transcendent world-view.

Furthermore, good quality education should aim to develop the personality of each student, stimulating his critical and creative abilities and preparing him to play a useful role in the life of society and the world of work. It should give everybody equal opportunities and select individuals to perform the different functions needed in society on the basis of their abilities and aptitudes. This means that good quality education should meet three requirements: democratization, social usefulness through a preparation for working life and a humanism that will prevent it from being governed exclusively by considerations of productivity. In this way, it will prepare for all-round development directed towards the harmonization of economic growth, social progress and culture; the aspirations of the individual; and the requirements of society.

Key factors affecting the quality of education

The curriculum

Together with educational structures, the curriculum, the level of teacher education and research are crucial to the quality of education. In his discussion of the curriculum, L. D'Hainaut[1] cites W. P. Siegel who found twenty-seven different definitions or descriptions of the curriculum in various works on education. D'Hainaut then proceeds to offer his own definition of the curriculum as an educational blueprint which embraces: (a) the aims and objectives of education; (b) the procedures, means and activities implemented to achieve these aims; and (c) the methods and instruments used to evaluate the extent to which the educational objectives have been achieved.

On the question of the curriculum, the conference noted that, although education in the region was no longer the preserve of selected élites and had been extended to the people at large, as well as being assigned a direct role in the socio-economic and cultural development of the countries and the democratization of society, those factors were not adequately reflected in the content, evaluation and promotion criteria or in school organization and teaching methods. Schools frequently did not fit into their social context and were lacking in communication mechanisms which would have enabled them to take account of the conditions and needs of the social and cultural environment. The democratization of education and the contribution it made to the development of the countries required educational content in keeping with the social interests and goals of the pupils and the role that they, their families and the communities in which they lived had to play in society. In this connection, mention was made of the limited place which knowledge of the social, economic and cultural realities of the various countries and of the region often occupies in curricula. This meant that education was irrelevant to the

1. L. D'Hainaut, 'Guiding Principles for Curriculum Development', *Curricula and Lifelong Education*, pp. 81–103, Paris, Unesco, 1981. (Education on the Move, 1.)

social milieu in which it was provided and did not, as any national education worthy of the name should, safeguard, cultivate and improve the distinctive cultural, historical and moral characteristics of the social milieu.

The final report of a meeting of experts on the Methodology of Curriculum Reform convened by Unesco in Paris in 1976 notes that a concern for relevance in the choice of objectives and in the preparation of the curricula deriving therefrom implies bringing education closer to life, to the natural and human environment and to the world of work, with the object of preparing the child or adolescent for his manifold responsibilities in a changing world, fitting the individual into his social environment and promoting national and cultural identity. This concern for relevance, which ensures that the child is not cut off from reality, helps to reduce failure and wastage. It should relate, at one and the same time, to the aspirations of individuals—children, young people and adults—and of the various social groups and to the requirements of society as a whole.

Educational needs have been widely discussed in educational literature. A. H. Maslow has developed an exceedingly straightforward and clear classification in which five categories of needs are identified: (a) primary needs (hunger, thirst, sexual needs); (b) the need for safety; (c) the need for integration; (d) the need for esteem; and (e) the need for fulfilment. It is evident that the first two categories of needs relate to survival or self-preservation, while the last three are social needs. In discussing profiles or the type of person to be educated, D'Hainaut[1] draws up a classification based on the different roles to be assumed by the individual in his private and family life, in his social life, his political life, his cultural life and his working life.

Content specification based on objectives, needs and aspirations is a complex task. It raises the perennial problem of what knowledge should be transmitted, what skills cultivated and what methods used, according to the age, level and ability of the pupil. The translation of overall objectives into content specification is first and foremost a matter for educationists and teachers, but it also requires the support and participation of specialists in different disciplines. One of the methods that may be used consists of expressing overall objectives in terms of pupil profiles at the different levels of the education system. These profiles, set out in terms of a taxonomy, provide a definition of the objectives to be attained in respect of knowledge, skills and attitudes.

It is interesting to note the essential features of good quality education which prepares for the future, as outlined by R. Jungk:[2]

increased accent on *creativity* and *discovery*,
increased accent on the permanent exercise of *critical faculties*,
increased accent on *preparation for participation* not only as a citizen but also in the economic sphere, the working environment,

1. D'Hainaut, op. cit.
2. Commentary by Dr R. Jungk, extracted from: Organisation for Economic Co-operation and Development (OECD), *Long-Range Policy Planning in Education*, pp. 224–5, Paris, OECD, 1973.

increased accent on *learning how to learn* (needed improvements of theory),

increased accent on *teaching of system and synergistic aspects* of knowledge ('seeing the whole', 'learning how to connect'),

the future possibilities of *educational technology* and the *limits* of such a technology as well as the dangers involved (education industries run by commercial firms or, what would be worse, ideological propagandists),

the future possibilities of *'gaming'* as an educational tool,

the future possibilities of *'direct learning'* (through travelling and first-hand experience),

the preparation for *coping with conflict*,

the preparation for *coping with change*,

the preparation for *living in an age of increasing population*, and consequently probable overcrowding.

Teacher-training and the quality of education

It has always been recognized that the teacher plays an important part in the provision of high-quality education: the training, selection and continuing in-service training of teachers are clearly major concerns in education, particularly when the quality of educational services is the focus of attention.

The conditions imposed on education by social, economic and political factors as well as by scientific and technical progress can significantly alter the role of the teacher, although some of his responsibilities and tasks remain essentially the same: thus, the teacher will always have an obligation to give his pupils an intellectual and moral training which assures and fosters both their personal development and their active integration into society.

Angel Oliveros has published an interesting work on the new functions of the educator[1] as compared with those that are unchanging. Among the traditional functions, Oliveros attaches primary importance to the task of imparting to the individual the knowledge, skills, customs, behaviour patterns and values of the society in which he was born (the process of socialization and enculturation). This involves a number of subordinate functions: the transmission of skills and knowledge (didactic function); the development of pupils' aptitudes (intellectual education); the inculcation of individual and social behaviour patterns (moral education); the inculcation of certain attitudes towards various realities of human life such as society (civic, democratic or social education), the human community (international education) and the family (family education). The second function involves helping the individual to discover his inner self and to achieve self-fulfilment (guidance function).

The manifold new functions of the educator, which reflect the age in which he lives, are more difficult to define than his traditional, unchanging functions. None the less, they can be said to include, according to Oliveros,

1. A. Oliveros, 'Lo permanente y lo nuevo en la formación del magisterio', *Proyecto Principal de Educación, Unesco–América Latina: Boletín Trimestral* (Havana, Unesco Regional Office for Culture in Latin America and the Caribbean), Vol. II, No. 7, July–September 1960, pp. 48–72.

helping the individual to discover and preserve his own personal values at the time of collective reactions and overwhelming propaganda; knowing and using various groups and the forces that spontaneously acquire an educational value in such groups; extending education to sectors and aspects of life which until now have had little contact with education; setting greater store by real-life experience than by academic learning; attaching greater value to the technical aspects of the education process and, consequently, the interconnections and interdependence between these aspects, as well as planning and evaluating the different stages of the education process in an appropriate way; and, lastly, preparing for an age of change.

These new requirements and those that can be expected to emerge over the next few decades call for constant improvements in the organization, content and methods of teacher education. The Special Intergovernmental Conference on the Status of Teachers, organized by Unesco in Paris in October 1966, saw teacher-training programmes in the following terms:

Teacher-preparation programmes

19. The purpose of a teacher-preparation programme should be to develop in each student his general education and personal culture, his ability to teach and educate others, an awareness of the principles which underlie good human relations, within and across national boundaries, and a sense of responsibility to contribute both by teaching and by example to social, cultural, and economic progress.
20. Fundamentally, a teacher-preparation programme should include:
    (a) general studies;
    (b) study of the main elements of philosophy, psychology, sociology as applied to education, the theory and history of education, and of comparative education, experimental pedagogy, school administration and methods of teaching the various subjects;
    (c) studies related to the student's intended field of teaching;
    (d) practice in teaching and in conducting extra-curricular activities under the guidance of fully qualified teachers.
21. (1) All teachers should be prepared in general, special and pedagogical subjects in universities, or in institutions on a level comparable to universities, or else in special institutions for the preparation of teachers.
    (2) The content of teacher-preparation programmes may reasonably vary according to the tasks the teachers are required to perform in different types of schools, such as establishments for handicapped children or technical and vocational schools. In the latter case, the programmes might include some practical experience to be acquired in industry, commerce or agriculture.
22. A teacher-preparation programme may provide for a professional course either concurrently with or subsequent to a course of personal academic or specialized education or skill cultivation.
23. Education for teaching should normally be full time; special arrangements may be made for older entrants to the profession and persons in other exceptional categories to undertake all or part of their course on a part-time basis, on condition that the content of such courses and the standards of attainment are on the same level as those of the full-time courses.
24. Consideration should be given to the desirability of providing for the education of different types of teachers, whether primary, secondary, technical, specialist or

vocational teachers, in institutions organically related or geographically adjacent to one another.

An original and interesting view of the contribution which a definite line of emphasis in teacher-training could make to the provision of equal opportunities is found in the work entitled *Social Influences on Educational Attainment* published by the OECD. According to this view, two aspects should be taken into account.

First, teacher-training should give more emphasis to the sociological and less to the didactic aspects of school education. As far as the didactic aspects are concerned, greater importance should be attached to individualized methods of instruction which make allowance for individual differences in social background. Part of an individualized attitude towards the teaching task is a 'diagnostic' orientation. Instead of spending a considerable time on checking the progress of individual pupils in relation to the rest of the class, the teacher should use this time for allowing the individual pupil's progress in relation to some absolute standard. Evaluation should therefore focus on the efficiency of the teaching and not so much on the relative competence attained by the pupils.

Second, the teaching cadre should be diversified in the sense that people other than certified teachers should be enlisted for classroom work. It would be advantageous if students while still in their teacher-training colleges could learn to collaborate with parents, asking them to come in and do part-time work, not only clerical and administrative chores but also actual teaching in small groups or by tutoring individual students. In addition to calling in such assistance, people of some achievement in the surrounding community should also be recruited to come to the teacher-training colleges from time to time and give expression to their experiences in their various chosen fields. This would counteract the isolation and the one-sided orientation towards didactic problems that has characterized teacher-training for so long.

The International Conference on Education, convened by Unesco, meeting in Geneva for its thirty-fifth session, from 27 August to 4 September 1975, set out in recommendation No. 69 concerning 'the changing role of the teacher and its influence on preparation for the profession and on in-service training' various underlying principles, including:

Whatever are or will be the changes in the education system, the teacher-learner relationship will remain at the centre of the educational process and therefore better preparation of educational personnel constitutes one of the essential factors of educational development and an important condition for any renovation in education.

In the section on 'the role of the teacher', the conference described various requirements connected with the teacher's role which reflect essential aspects of high-quality education at the present time:

Teachers and administrators of all categories and levels should be aware of the roles played by them in the present state and development of education. They should understand that their roles and functions are not fixed unchangeable categories, but are evolving under the influence of changes taking place in society and in the education system itself.

Despite the diversity of education systems and of arrangements for teacher education throughout the world, there is a general need for fresh national scrutiny, in a realistic manner, of the teachers' specific tasks and functions in terms of national policies and legislation. Such national analyses, with the participation of teachers themselves, should lead to the establishment of professional profiles for all categories of teachers and other educational personnel with clear definitions of the roles and functions assigned to them by the society.

Measures should be taken to ensure that conditions exist for serving teachers and future teachers to be aware of the changes in the teacher's role and to be prepared for new roles and functions.

The teacher is engaged more and more today in the implementation of new educational procedures, taking advantage of all the resources of modern educational devices and methods. He is an educator and a counsellor who tries to develop his pupils' abilities and interests and not merely to serve as a source of information and a transmitter of knowledge; the teacher plays a principal role in providing his pupils with a scientific world outlook.

Since the role of the school is no longer limited to instruction, the teacher, apart from his instructional duties, has now to assume more responsibility, in collaboration with other educational agents in the community, for the preparation of the young for community life, family life, productive activity, etc. The teacher should have more opportunity for involvement in extra-curricular and out-of-school activities, in guiding and counselling the pupils and their parents, and in organizing his pupils' leisure-time activities.

Teachers should be aware of the important role they are called upon to play in the local community as professionals and citizens, as agents of development and change and be given the possibility of practising that role.

It should be recognized that the effectiveness of school education depends largely upon the development of new relationships between the teacher and his pupils, who become more active partners in the education process; between the teacher and his colleagues and other agents who may be called upon to co-operate with him; between the teacher and his pupils' parents and others in the community concerned with the process of education.

The in-service training of teachers

In the context of the quality of education, the conference recognized the vital importance of providing further training for teachers. In fact, while periodic retraining is needed today in a wide range of professions and occupations in view of scientific and technological progress, the advance of knowledge and the development of teaching methods and techniques make lifelong education particularly necessary in the teaching profession. The need for such training is obviously more acute for unqualified and untrained teachers. However, even for suitably trained personnel, the teacher-training course should be regarded as only the initial or first phase of a continuing process.

An all-round programme of further training for teachers should obviously help them to lead a richer cultural life. However, any consideration of this point should be based on the need, as Kandel maintained, for the educator to cease to be a being-for-himself and become a being-for-others. The man-in-the-street learns in order to know. The professional person learns in order to apply his knowledge to specific problems arising in the course of his work. But the teacher learns in order to pass his knowledge on to others. None the less, it would be very restrictive, indeed narrow-minded, to think in terms of limiting the teacher's knowledge—as in fact occurs in some cases—strictly to the content of the syllabus. It would seem to be a statement of the obvious to maintain that the teacher has to know more than he actually teaches. Unfortunately, however, this is not always the case in schools. The teacher is sometimes considered to be performing his duty and to be fully qualified when he has mastered no more than the knowledge contained in the syllabus he has to organize. At first sight, this would not seem to present the teacher with any great problem. In point of fact, however, the task of determining what must be covered and what is not strictly necessary for a given course or grade is an extremely arduous task.

Furthermore, if the teacher's knowledge is strictly limited he is unlikely to be capable of imaginative teaching or a creative approach to learning. This lack of broad knowledge will also debar him from one of the most rewarding aspects of his work, namely guiding gifted pupils by opening up new vistas for them in subjects in which they have a special interest. Likewise, mastery of a subject and a broad grasp of its significance and implications provide, as Hernández Ruiz has said, the best educational basis for lively, relaxed, interesting teaching. If the teacher is lacking in general education, teaching becomes a distressing burden, revealing uncertainties and gaps in his knowledge, which are disheartening for teacher and pupil alike. It is interesting to note, in this connection, with particular reference to the teachers' social position or image, that the pedantry so often attributed to the primary-school teacher derives in no small degree from the shallowness of his knowledge.

Examination of the teaching profession's qualifications reveals that many thousands of teachers have only attended primary school or part of the secondary course. The requirement set out at the beginning of this section, that the teacher should know far more than he is going to teach his pupils, is thus far from being satisfied. If one also bears in mind the desire of all the countries in the region to extend the length of compulsory schooling, and the implications of this measure in terms of improved content and a higher level of knowledge, the seriousness of the problem to be tackled by in-service teacher-training schemes is easily appreciated.

Passing from the specific problem of the least well-qualified teacher, we find that the same principle also applies, although, naturally, to a lesser degree, to the teacher who has undergone a systematic course of training in a teacher-training establishment. While the need to update and broaden knowledge continually is common to all professions, it is an essential aspect of teacher-training.

A number of conclusions may be drawn from these considerations. First, it is practically pointless to recruit teachers lacking a sound general education unless immediate and continuous steps are taken to provide them with such a background. Another point concerns the direction to be given to this general training if teachers are to be trained to 'act' and not merely to think. A third conclusion concerns the need to find ways of encouraging the teacher to undertake practical research—in connection with educational situations and their causes—on the basis of his own observation and thinking rather than on the basis of bookish monographs consisting mainly of references to other works. The teacher has to learn how to teach; he has to master some of the techniques used to impart knowledge. While teacher-training establishments and institutes of education give some guidelines and broad directions, and can even provide an opportunity for a certain amount of actual teaching practice, of varying degrees of usefulness, they cannot give the prospective teacher a training that will provide the answer to all his problems. The practical realities of school life, the range of needs and interests of individual pupils and the complexities inherent in the job itself, which continually present the teacher with new, unforeseen situations, mean that his educational knowledge has to be constantly improved. He also needs to be kept informed of developments and advances in educational techniques.

But in this extremely important area of further training for teachers, which is concerned with techniques used specifically in the teaching profession, a good deal of progress still needs to be made and the most appropriate course of action is not always adopted. It is not uncommon to hear a newly qualified teacher criticize the training college for providing a purely theoretical knowledge which is of little use in solving the everyday problems of school life. This kind of criticism seems particularly common when an attempt is made to introduce activity methods, interdisciplinary approaches or self-expression among pupils, for example, without providing—and this, sad to relate, is usually the case—a sound basis of practical training with first-class teachers, which enables the student to assimilate teaching techniques as no mere statement of principle or theory can. In such cases, the new teacher becomes a prey to one of the scourges of the teaching profession: a profoundly sceptical attitude to new teaching methods.

If the training provided in teacher-training establishments occasionally produces the kind of results we have observed, will there not be a danger of the same mistakes being repeated if further training schemes are run along similar lines? The fact is that both the courses currently organized to train unqualified teachers and the procedures generally adopted for in-service training for qualified teachers suffer from many of the shortcomings of the teacher-training system, particularly the lack of practical training.

There is also a need for careful consideration, during the development of specific further-training programmes for teachers, of the fact that, while it is accepted that the improvement of the teacher's performance should be based primarily on a study of practical situations taken from the everyday life of the school, it should also be borne in mind that any such improvement must not be derived solely from practical considerations, whose value to the teacher is relatively short-lived.

The further training of teachers should be conceived in terms of a broad range of options and subjects and involve the inspectorate, teacher-training institutions and scientific and cultural institutions, teachers' organizations and documentation centres. Further training should be provided in a variety of forms: traditional courses, lectures and seminars, study groups, exchange schemes, special study leave and the circulation of documentation.

With a view to encouraging the active participation of the profession in further-training schemes, it would be necessary to introduce certain promotional incentives which should include access to various management posts or specialized jobs linked to appropriate courses of study. Today, an effective education system needs a variety of special skills if it is to meet, as it should, the manifold demands on education (school psychologists, teachers for special schools, specialists in educational technology, principals and school inspectors, etc.).

Research

It is with some dismay that Piaget, when discussing educational research, asks the following question:

So why is pedagogy so little the work of pedagogues? This is a serious and ever-present problem. The general problem is to understand why the vast army of educators now labouring throughout the entire world with such devotion and, in general, with such competence, does not engender an élite of researchers capable of making pedagogy into a discipline, at once scientific and alive, that could take its rightful place among all those other applied disciplines that draw upon both art and science.[1]

Piaget's point is graphically borne out by the fact that the pioneers of systematic educational research were not professional educators in the strict sense of the term. Suffice it to recall the names of Decroly and Maria Montessori who, like Clarapède, were doctors. There are a number of reasons for this phenomenon. One is the conviction, which is still widely held, that teaching is a menial task that does not need to be based on scientific principles. Another is the fact that teacher-training does not attach sufficient importance to the development of an inquiring frame of mind. Other reasons are the lack of contact between research centres and teachers, and the notorious shortage of research funds.

The attitude to educational research could be summed up as a lack of interest or faith in either the need for or the value of this activity, which betrays considerable ignorance of the complexity of the educational process. Educational research has an extremely important part to play in education policy-making and planning, as well as in such aspects of education as the study of the different stages in the psychological and biological development of the pupil; different rates and patterns of learning; the structure of education

1. Jean Piaget, *Science of Education and the Psychology of the Child*, London, Longman, 1971.

systems; educational content and teaching methods; school organization; the effects of rapid social change on eduation, educational guidance and vocational guidance; the use of new educational technology; and, naturally, the knowledge of and methods of teaching the different subjects and activities which have to be provided. The establishment of a close relationship between research and teaching, and between research and education policy-making is a prerequisite for improving the measurable efficiency of education systems and the quality of the education which they provide.

In Latin America, since the Conference of Ministers of Education and Those Responsible for the Promotion of Science and Technology organized by Unesco in Venezuela in 1971, interest in research into education has increased : regional meetings have been convened, by Unesco or by individual research centres or foundations, in Buenos Aires, Santiago, Mexico City and São Paulo, and new research institutes have been established and old ones rejuvenated. At the first of these meetings, the educational-research situation in the region was summed up as follows:[1]

Educational research is going forward in all the countries, whether in institutes specially established for that purpose, in university faculties and institutes of education, in technical services of the education authorities or in educational planning offices in both the public and the private sector.

The research carried out is extremely limited in content and scope and in the main reflects the particular interests of the persons or institutions concerned, which work in isolation. None the less, a tendency to gear research to the general educational problems and needs in the different countries is now emerging. This tendency stems from the efforts of the Latin American countries to formulate policies and set out effective education plans based on objective knowledge of the situation and educational requirements. These countries do not yet have a fully co-ordinated system, an effective policy, or research activities which are implemented according to an order of priorities and geared to the problems and needs of educational development at both national and regional level.

Research departments are under-staffed, with personnel who are, in the main, not specifically trained for research work and do not cover the broad range of subjects needed for interdisciplinary teams. Furthermore, career incentives for educational research workers are sadly lacking.

The financial resources earmarked for educational research in both national budgets and the budgets of other institutions, including those of the international agencies, are extremely limited and do not reflect the magnitude of the task or the importance now attached to research.

This description of the situation in educational research in Latin America suggests that there are inadequacies in three important areas: the type of research work done, the lack of qualified personnel and the shortage of research funds.

Educational research will only yield results if the type of research needed

1. Donald Lemke, *La investigación educacional en Latinoamérica y el Caribe: una visión histórica*, Santiago de Chile, Unesco Regional Office for Education in Latin America and the Caribbean, 1975, 24 pp.

and the conditions required for success are correctly assessed. In a lecture he gave at Stanford University, Professor Bush described these as follows:

1. Educational research must deal with the educational system as a whole and not small segments taken in artificial isolation; 2. unless there is a team of research workers at each of three levels—national, institutional and specific— the battle will be in effect lost from the start; 3. educational research which is not completely interdisciplinary is stillborn; 4. research must start in the classroom and stay there, without neglecting basic theoretical work; 5. measures must be taken to ensure that research findings are widely publicized and—for this is by no means the same thing—put into practice. We must also bear in mind that research work will starve to death if it does not get feedback from the school system, and if it is not itself committed to continuing evaluation of its usefulness. Without concertation with schools, without co-ordination and without some division of labour our efforts will be in vain. For what we need is what could be called an open management system for educational research. I should also like to point out that if research is still not an integral part of the educational system this is because that system has not yet made enough progress in the scientific field.

The positive and effective provision of these conditions calls for consideration of some of the approaches to or forms of organization of educational research. Above all, a distinction should be drawn between educational or organizational innovations, introduced by various teachers or educational establishments, with a comparatively limited scope, and research conducted by interdisciplinary teams (of psychologists, sociologists, economists and educators, for example) who, in the framework of special institutions or education workshops, carry out a centralized form of research which is frequently unrelated to practical realities in the schools.

Both kinds of research are necessary and they are, in fact, complementary; however, they have to be linked, and one possible way of doing this would be to grant a broad measure of initiative and independence to various educational establishments, whose experiments would be co-ordinated and their results monitored and evaluated by an institution such as an education faculty or a body created to encourage innovation in education.

To this end, encouragement should be given to activities involving experimentation and the introduction in educational establishments of educational innovations, whether suggested by research establishments or independently devised and developed in the educational establishments themselves.

The Mexico City Conference highlighted the need to strengthen national research centres and recommended that Unesco establish a regional co-operation network for educational innovations. When implementing this recommendation, close examination of the work done in Asia since 1975 within the framework of the Unesco programme could be extremely useful.

The Asian Centre of Educational Innovation for Development was established in this region as part of Unesco's Regional Office for Education in Asia and Oceania. This centre was set up with the aim of fostering educational innovation. It provides technical and advisory services, promotes and facilitates the exchange and pooling of experience and provides information on educational innovations.

These activities are implemented through a network of centres and national projects which have been associated with the above centre. These associated centres organize regional, subregional and national training courses. They also carry out the following activities:

New orientations and structures in education. This involves experimentation with new education structures, in-school and out-of-school, as well as identifying unused and under-utilized educational resources.

Management of educational innovations. Special attention is given to the development and management of innovative activities undertaken in other sectors, to co-operation between institutions and within the institutions themselves, and to an interdisciplinary approach.

Curriculum development. This encourages innovative approaches, methods, materials and techniques designed to make education relevant to national development objectives.

Educational technology. Emphasis is placed on the opportunities offered by educational technology for the development of education, taking into account different aspects of and problems in education.

New structures and methods in teacher training. This concerns the promotion of an integrated approach to pre-service and in-service training for formal and non-formal education, as well as the renewal of structures, methods and programmes for teacher-training and teacher-educator training.

Science education. Particular attention is devoted to the growing importance of science in all aspects of daily life, to the expansion of agricultural and industrial production and to the improvement of living conditions.

While we felt it useful to give this illustration of work done in other regions it is obvious that the specific nature of educational problems in Latin America and the Caribbean, as well as the region's own experience in the field of educational research, call for an approach to the implementation of the recommendation of the Mexico City Conference which may differ considerably from the Asian approach in regard to both the priority research areas and the structure of the network of educational innovations. At one of the meetings on educational research in Latin America sponsored by Unesco, the following themes were considered to be of particular significance in the region: the validity and achievement of educational objectives, educational structure and content, the efficiency of the systems, the financing and cost of education, teaching methods, school organization, the bio-psychological and socio-economic characteristics of the pupils, and educational and vocational guidance.

Obviously, the effectiveness of research will ultimately depend on its results being disseminated and gradually put into practice by educational establishments. For this the most appropriate information media should be used (seminars, publications, video cassettes, etc.) and an effort should be made to attract the interest of teachers with a view to associating them with research work: unless teachers feel that they are involved in research in some way, it is extremely difficult for research workers to have their findings generally accepted and applied by teachers. This vital *rapprochement* and co-operation between research workers and teachers will only be possible if, among other things, research studies deal with genuine problems encountered in the everyday life of educational establishments, if the teachers are sufficiently trained to understand the findings and the terminology of the research workers, and if the latter are prepared to frame their statements and guidelines in simpler and more accessible language.

Quantitative objectives
for the year 2000

The extension of compulsory schooling:
real possibilities

One of the goals set for education systems in the Mexico City Declaration is the provision of a minimum of eight to ten years' general education for all school-age children. This goal reflects a tendency that is already apparent in a number of Latin American countries, as mentioned above.

The extension of the duration of schooling needs very little justification. Until recently, the primary school was, in most countries, the only school to which the least-privileged sectors of society had any access. This made primary education seem complete in itself, and not one stage leading to another, except for those able to surmount the barrier barring access to secondary education. Nowadays, even the most elementary occupations require far more in terms of maturity and knowledge than the primary school can offer. Furthermore, the fact that advances and changes in the technological processes of production call for a multi-purpose training is beginning radically to change attitudes to the nature and limitations of schooling. The need to provide for a longer period of school education will lead to changes in the structure of the education system, in the level of teacher-education and in curricula and programmes of study. Various disciplines or subjects, among other elements, will have to be broadened, with a view to meeting the requirements of this extended period of general education.

For this objective to be attained, two things will have to be done. On the one hand, legislation concerning the duration of compulsory schooling will have to be amended and provision made for the necessary resources in terms of personnel, buildings, equipment, etc.; on the other, effective assistance should be provided for students throughout the entire period of their education.

What is the likelihood of such objectives being attained? The answer to this question is necessarily based on estimates and hedged about with reservations since, in an undertaking of this nature, various factors have to be taken into consideration: political decision-making, the current level of schooling and the availability of financial resources, apart from the requirements set out in the preceding paragraph.

If the current level of schooling is taken as an indication, the likelihood of achieving this goal varies considerably from country to country. One group of countries (Argentina, Barbados, Chile, Costa Rica, Cuba, Guyana, Jamaica, Mexico, Panama) has over 90 per cent enrolment in the 6-to-11 age-group, while in a number of these countries enrolment is 100 per cent. In another group (Bolivia, Brazil, Dominican Republic, Ecuador, Paraguay, Peru and Venezuela), there is between 75 and 90 per cent enrolment. In a third group (Colombia, El Salvador, Guatemala, Haiti, Honduras and Nicaragua) enrolment is below 75 per cent.

The enrolment of the 6-to-11 age-group is not a major problem in the great majority of countries; in fact, a number of countries have already solved it. In other countries, persistence, without any significant expenditure, is all that is needed to achieve the goal. The least promising situations are those found in Guatemala, Haiti, Honduras and El Salvador, now that Nicaragua has adopted new policies for the rapid expansion of primary education. It is doubtful whether these countries can effectively attain the objective without considerable sacrifices at national level and significant international support because, among other reasons, apart from the shortfall in enrolment that has to be made up, they all have a high rate of population increase.

The provision of school education for the 11-plus age-group represents a far greater problem. Nevertheless, around a third of the countries have already achieved over 70 per cent enrolment in the 12-to-17 age-group. Although this percentage obviously includes a fair number of repeaters, it is also certain that the increase in the duration of schooling proposed in the Mexico City Declaration would involve not only pupils staying at school after the normal age-limit of 17 if they had started school at the age of 8 or thereabouts, or had repeated grades at some stage. None the less, another third of the countries, composed, naturally, of those with the greatest shortfalls in primary education, will be unable to achieve the proposed goal of eight to nine years' schooling without a very substantial improvement on the trend recorded in recent years. For it should be borne in mind that many thousands of children in rural areas at present receive no more than two or three years' schooling.

In all cases—countries that will find it quite easy to achieve the proposed target, countries at an intermediate stage and backward countries—there will be a need for concerted action involving the planning of the gradual expansion and extension of the education system and also financing. This action should be based on firm policy decisions taken with a view to achieving the proposed objective, in full in a good number of the countries of the region and to a significant degree in those which are very unlikely to be able to achieve it fully.

Such action will undoubtedly have repercussions on the structure of the education system. Until now the duration of compulsory schooling has been identified with the duration of primary education. At the end of primary school, three possibilities were generally open: (a) to start work; (b) to learn a trade at a vocational training centre; or (c) to start a course of secondary education. There are a number of possible formulae for extending the period of compulsory schooling. One is to maintain the traditional distinction between primary and secondary education, and to introduce a compulsory period of secondary education. Another approach is to design a common core to be taught in one school in such a way that the two levels are merged into a single period of education, followed by a new level equivalent to the second phase of secondary education. This formula has already been adopted in a number of countries under the name of basic general education. Apart from offering the pupils a more complete education, one of the advantages of this formula is that it defers any 'dividing of the ways' in education until the decision on whether to continue with 'academic' studies or to go into vocational training in the strict sense of the term. This represents an advance in terms of achieving equality of opportunity.

The eradication of illiteracy

One of the major objectives set in the Mexico City Declaration is to eradicate illiteracy by the end of the century. Despite the efforts made, it has not yet been possible to realize this long-standing aspiration of the countries of Latin America.

A number of literacy schools were established in Brazil as far back as 1889. In the second decade of this century, post-revolutionary Mexico decided to extend the benefits of education to all strata of the population. In El Salvador, various efforts were made in this direction in 1919, while a literacy campaign was launched in Ecuador in 1934 by the National Union of Journalists. Similar activities have been carried out in various other Latin American countries.

Since 1940, more resolute efforts have been made to eradicate illiteracy and in various countries official bodies have been established to manage literacy action (in Chile and Mexico in 1944, Ecuador in 1945, Brazil in 1947, Colombia in 1948, Costa Rica in 1949 and Honduras in 1950).

These different initiatives add up to a continental movement in the sense that they all involve similar criteria and procedures. International co-operation in the attainment of these aims was also introduced. Unesco established the Regional Centre for Fundamental Education in Pázcuaro (Mexico) to train community education advisers using an approach adapted to the requirements imposed by the particular characteristics of the Latin American rural environment and giving broad emphasis in its activities to adult literacy training. The seminars in Caracas (1948) and Rio de Janeiro (1949), which were convened by the OAS and held with the participation of Unesco, were effective in helping to foster public awareness of the problem of illiteracy. They also laid the bases and set out valuable guidelines for the development of literacy campaigns. In addition, help was provided by experts on Unesco's technical assistance missions in the organization of these campaigns in different Latin American countries, particularly through functional literacy projects.

TABLE 15. Illiterates in the population aged 15 and over in Latin America and the Caribbean

Illiteracy rate (%)	1980			1990		
	Country	illiterates aged 15 and over (thousands)	Average rate (%)	Country	illiterates aged 15 and over (thousands)	Average rate (%)
Over 50	Haiti	2 125.5	71.3	Haiti	2 331.2	64.5
40 to 50	Guatemala	1 885.7	47.3	—	—	—
25 to 40	Bolivia	1 286.0		Bolivia	1 172.2	
	Dominican Republic	835.4		El Salvador	998.3	
	El Salvador	930.6		Guatemala	1 985.4	
	Honduras	598.2		Nicaragua	515.3	
	Nicaragua	475.5				
		4 125.7	32.6		4 671.2	29.6
10 to 25	Brazil	18 141.3		Brazil	15 857.6	
	Colombia	2 295.2		Dominican		
	Ecuador	850.6		Republic	857.0	
	Mexico	6 139.4		Ecuador	762.3	
	Panama	160.0		Honduras	589.7	
	Paraguay	243.5		Paraguay	235.0	
	Peru	1 842.4		Peru	1 495.8	
	Venezuela	1 453.5		Venezuela	1 385.0	
		31 125.9	20.1		21 182.4	15.1
Less than 10	Argentina	1 293.8		Argentina	1 387.9	
	Chile	558.6		Chile	444.9	
	Costa Rica	97.3		Colombia	1 747.4	
	Guyana	23.6		Costa Rica	69.9	
	Jamaica	57.1		Guyana	21.1	
	Trinidad and Tobago	31.5		Jamaica	70.6	
				Mexico	4 822.2	
				Panama	135.7	
				Trinidad and Tobago	27.0	
		2 061.9	6.7		8 726.7	7.6
TOTAL		41 324.7			36 911.5	
General average rate			20.2			13.4

Source: *Estimates and Projections of Illiteracy*, Paris, Unesco, 1978. (Current Studies and Research in Statistics, CSR. E29.)

But despite these unremitting labours which, in a number of countries, such as Cuba, have produced very satisfactory results, illiteracy rates are still high.

The present situation and foreseeable trends are shown in Table 15. If the trend which emerges from these figures is confirmed, it may be concluded that the objective set in the Mexico City Declaration can be achieved, almost completely, by the end of the century, by two-thirds of the countries of the region. It will, however, be necessary, in various countries, to change the approach pursued until now.

First, it is obvious that universal school attendance is, in the long run, the most effective method, in so far as it checks the growth of illiteracy and, gradually, reduces the number of illiterates. But this will only come about if the period of school education is long enough; a short, minimal period of schooling, such as is the norm in the most rural areas, is insufficient, particularly if account is taken of the shortage, in such areas, of reading material and other resources which would help pupils to retain the knowledge and skills they have acquired. In this connection, it is interesting to note in Table 15 that in countries with high enrolment ratios—and not only those that have achieved them recently—the illiteracy rate has dropped less than might have been expected.

If the objective stated in the Mexico City Declaration is to be achieved, the only way to tackle the illiteracy problem is to use unconventional means. These may involve the large-scale mobilization of the population with a view to drastically bringing down illiteracy rates within the shortest possible time. This model has been applied in Cuba and is now being applied in Nicaragua. Another method is the MOBRAL method (Brazil) which provides for vocational training together with literacy training and tends to take in community-development work as well. Whichever of these approaches is used, literacy training will only have a lasting effect if it is followed up by extensive post-literacy programmes which will also require very substantial funds.

The gradual increase in education budgets

The Mexico City Declaration stated that the countries of the region should gradually increase their education budgets until they are allocating not less than 7 or 8 per cent of GNP to their education systems.

It is by no means easy to assess the chances of achieving this objective. Indeed, such an assessment can only be made with many qualifications and reservations. Many different factors are involved, and it is particularly difficult to predict economic trends and infer from them implications for educational funding. J. K. Galbraith was not far from the mark when he jokingly claimed that economists are singularly well qualified to analyse past economic trends but less well qualified to predict the future. What is more, economists are not the only ones of whom this is true.

One difficulty is the lack of completely reliable data on the proportion of

GNP allocated by the various countries for education and on its growth over recent decades, since both of these are important factors in establishing estimates. The reports available on this subject are, in general, based exclusively on public expenditure and do not take into account the contributions—in some countries extremely significant—made by the private sector and, in particular, by families, local agencies or bodies or other ministries.

Table 16 shows a classification of the countries of the region based on the percentage of public expenditure represented by education in 1976. Despite its unquestionable usefulness, this table suffers from the inadequacies mentioned above.

TABLE 16. Latin America and the Caribbean. Classification of countries according to public expenditure on education as a percentage of GNP in 1976

Less than 3%	3–3.9%	4–4.9%	5–5.9%	6–7%	Over 7%
Argentina[1]	Bolivia	Ecuador[2]	Grenada	Costa Rica	Barbados
Brazil	Chile[1]	Honduras	Suriname[1]	Guyana	Cuba[3]
Dominican	El Salvador	Mexico	Venezuela	Jamaica	
Republic	Peru	Panama			
Guatemala	Trinidad				
Haiti	and Tobago				
Nicaragua					
Paraguay					

1. 1975.   2. 1977.   3. 9.9%, 1974.

Source: Quantitative Evolution Projections of Enrolment in the Educational Systems of Latin America and the Caribbean. Statistical Analysis (ED-79/MINEDLAC/Ref. 2). (Document prepared by the Unesco Secretariat for the Conference of Ministers of Education held in Mexico City, 4–13 December 1979.)

Table 16 shows that public expenditure on education (budget) represented more than 7 per cent of GNP in only two countries (Barbados and Cuba) and more than 6 per cent in only five countries (the preceding two countries and Costa Rica, Guyana and Jamaica).

It is observed, furthermore, that in several countries with comparatively favourable education indicators, public expenditure on education represents a low percentage of GNP in terms of the stated objective. This is the case in Argentina, Chile and Uruguay (3.6 per cent in 1970).

The question may also be viewed in economic terms. In several of the countries where public expenditure on education is under 5 per cent of GNP, which means that they are those farthest from achieving the target set in the Mexico City Declaration, the per capita domestic product is, in both absolute and relative terms, below average for the countries of the region. This is the case of Haiti, Paraguay, Bolivia and Honduras.

Some countries consider that it will not be easy to improve upon the very considerable economic effort put into education in recent years. None the less, expenditure on education in Latin America as a whole is lower than in other regions. In a study prepared by Ortiz Mena, director of the Inter-American Development Bank, for a meeting held at Harvard in 1973, it was stated that in 1970, Latin America spent on education around 3.3 per cent of its GDP, or the equivalent of $4,800 million. The world average, expressed as a percentage of GNP, came to 5.4 per cent in 1966.

Ortiz Mena then quoted 1970 enrolment figures for the Latin American countries which showed that around 30.2 million children in the 6-to-12 age-group were enrolled in elementary education; 9.6 million adolescents in the 12-to-18 age-group were attending courses of higher education.

He went on to say that, taking into account the rate of increase over the last decade, it had been estimated that in 1980 there would be 50.4 million primary-school pupils, 26.1 million secondary-school students and 4.5 million university students. By 1990 or thereabouts, there would be 83.1 million primary-school pupils, 51.9 million secondary-school students and 11.2 million university students. Finally, by the year 2000, the number of students at the three levels would be 110.2, 73.6 and 24.4 million respectively. In other words, by the end of the twentieth century, Latin America would have succeeded in providing universal primary education—something it had wanted to do since the nineteenth century—and in achieving enrolment ratios in secondary and higher education approaching those already achieved now in the United States. He felt that this could hardly be considered gratifying in times of such rapid historical change and revolution in consumer expectations.

On the basis of the cost per dollar per pupil per year, estimated at $82 for primary-school pupils, $135 for secondary-school students and $625 for students in higher education, and taking into account the above-mentioned enrolment increases, without altering the average expenditure as given above (which is unrealistic, since educational expenditure tends to increase more rapidly), Ortiz Mena pointed out that the amounts shown in Table 17 would be required to finance education in Latin America over the next few years.

TABLE 17. Amounts required to finance education in the region (in constant 1970 dollars)

Year	$ millions	Period	Annual rate of real growth
1975	7 030	1975–80	8.4
1980	10 495	1980–85	8.6
1985	15 830	1985–90	5.7
1990	20 895	1990–95	5.2
1995	26 820	1995–2000	4.9
2000	34 105		
		1975–2000	6.5

Source: Ortiz Mena, *Estudios sobre gastos en educación*, 1973.

As Ortiz Mena himself points out, the above hypothesis could be modified by a variety of factors; they include the level of teachers' pay (which is currently low), the shortage of qualified teachers, the need for a substantial increase in the number of teachers, the construction of school buildings and the allocation of school furniture and teaching materials.

A considerable effort will therefore be needed to achieve the increase in the percentage of GNP allocated for education defined at the Mexico City Conference as essential for the expansion and improvement of education systems. This effort should be made in two directions: on the one hand, the use of a reasonable share of any economic growth to finance education; on the other, greater rationalization of educational expenditure.

The prospects do not appear unfavourable as far as the first point is concerned. According to a report presented by Ortiz Mena at a meeting of the Inter-American Development Bank held in Rio de Janeiro in April 1980, the GNP of the countries of the region had risen, in 1979, by around 6 per cent, allowing for inflation, as compared with an average increase between 1975 and 1978 of approximately 4.3 per cent. The 1979 increase in GNP had thus been the largest since the 1973/74 oil crisis, returning to the levels recorded over the 1960–73 period.

The most developed countries had derived the greatest benefit from this situation. Argentina, which had recorded a negative rate of 3.2 per cent in 1978, had shown an improvement of 7 per cent in 1979. Brazil and Mexico both had growth rates varying between 6 and 8 per cent. In Peru, where the growth-rate had been zero in 1977 and regressed by 0.7 per cent in 1978, GNP had risen by around 3 per cent. However, there was a vast difference between the poorest country, Haiti, where the average per capita annual income was around $200, and the richest country, Venezuela, where the per capita annual income was $2,100.

On the occasion of the twentieth anniversary of the Inter-American Development Bank, Ortiz Mena presented a resolutely optimistic review of the last two decades, pointing out that during that period, Latin America had evolved, modernized itself and developed; and that the Inter-American Development Bank had played an important part in this process, acting as a catalyst in the mobilization of national and international resources for development. The considerable progress made in the region had enabled Latin Americans to enjoy a better standard of living than twenty years previously and to have much easier access to medical care and other basic social services.

Over the last twenty years, GNP in the South American continent has practically trebled, rising from $149 billion to $430 billion (constant). By way of comparison, this figure represented, in 1979, some 8 per cent of the total GNP of the developed countries as against 6 per cent in 1960. Industry has been the driving force behind this improvement, particularly in Brazil, Mexico and Argentina, in that order. Latin America currently produces more than half the Third World's manufactured goods.

In the second direction mentioned, that of rationalization, a determined effort is needed to increase educational efficiency. Despite the evident improvements, there is a lamentable waste of energy and considerable mismanagement, which should be reduced through improved educational technology but also, and primarily, by adapting education more effectively to socio-economic realities, and to the needs, possibilities and aspirations which reflect them.

Proven productivity is a prerequisite for maintaining and, even more, for increasing educational investment and operating expenditure, one of the most characteristic trends in the development of the modern economy. It is not enough to point to the needs of the pupils and students; it must also be shown that educators and administrators are competent.

The education of the least-privileged social groups

Rural population

In the section on rural education, mention was made of some of the problems encountered in this area of education which, broadly speaking, may be summed up as discrimination in terms of equality of opportunity and the poor adaptation of the type of education provided to development. Closely associated with this problem is the situation of the groups which inhabit the poverty belts around the large towns, formed mainly of migrants from rural areas.

Experience in the promotion of rural education clearly indicates that its success will be extremely limited unless it is closely combined with very far-reaching programmes of social change.

In certain areas of the rural environment, there is a clear appreciation of the need for such processes of transformation to include changes in patterns of land tenure, an increase in production and employment levels, a more equitable distribution of income, the creation of local processing industries for agricultural products, the expansion of local trade, the provision of loans, the improvement of roads and communications, the extension of health and hygiene services, improvements in nutrition and housing standards, and support for systems of local self-government and community co-operation schemes.

Such reforms can only be achieved if overall development plans include detailed and wide-ranging rural-development programmes. No substantial improvement in the situation of the human groups who live in this environment will be possible unless policies are adopted to decentralize industry, to give an impetus to key development areas, to strengthen national infrastructures in the interior by setting up development zones or regions through multi-sectoral measures, and to decentralize public investment.

The primary objective of these measures should be to wipe out differences between essential welfare services and living conditions in rural areas and in the cities of the region.

The role played by education in this context is fundamental. But what type of education should it be? An interesting answer to this question is found in the report presented by the Peruvian delegation to the Mexico City Conference:

Educational reform in Peru is making an extremely important contribution to the promotion of the rural population in terms both of its overall approach and of its ways of tackling educational problems in these areas. In terms of its overall approach, it establishes the need to avoid any distinction between rural education and education in the cities, seeing that the system is unified and homogeneous; there should, however, be a distinctive form of education for rural areas, which provides opportunities for horizontal and vertical social mobility.

This approach has a number of implications, such as the need

to offer general knowledge and all-round training to all students, with the provision, at the same time, of instruction enabling them to understand the environment in which they live, to play a conscious and active part in it and to help to solve its problems; in other words education of a type which caters just as much for the needs of those who remain in the rural environment as those who leave it. All this will require a form of planning that integrates or co-ordinates education for children, young people and adults, both in and out of school, and links government action with that of the communities themselves. Another requirement, moreover, is the systematic definition of the content of education, of the various categories of teachers and their training and of the most suitable forms of educational organization for the efficient development of education in rural areas.

The conference recommended the following criteria and lines of approach to states:

That they guarantee, within the context of the all-round training of the individual, general education and vocational and specialized training offering equality of opportunity in respect both of access and numerical coverage of pupils and of the quality and level of preparation which the education system should provide, the whole system being adapted to the features of the environment in which it operates;

That they ensure the provision, in teacher education plans, through application of the principle of combining study and work, of adequate training for teaching staff so that the work they perform will be of the same level in rural zones as in urban areas;

That they assign priority, in education plans for rural development, to objectives relating to the provision, in the long term, of:

(a) complete elementary or primary education for all school-age children;

(b) basic general education, secondary level or incomplete secondary education, at the first stage, and complete general secondary education at a subsequent stage; consideration should be given, in this respect, to Member States' ability to implement the principle of combining study with productive work among students in educational boarding establishments, and thus to help finance the extension of such services, a principle which, in addition, makes an invaluable contribution to the all-round development of the pupil's personality;

(c) literacy training for adults and young people;

That they analyse the possibility of the creation and strengthening by Member States of scholarship schemes for students in rural areas which will ensure the real provision of education completely free of expense, with a view to guaranteeing the access of children and young people in rural areas to secondary and higher educational establishments in the national system. The Member States should also study the possibility of setting up a system of educational loans for students in higher education.

That they engage in research, promote studies and experiment with work training programmes for young people and adults living in rural areas and marginal urban zones;

That they draw up and implement integrated programmes on nutrition, health, basic rural sanitation and housing which will provide adults with a personalized education enabling them to receive training for work in keeping with their personal aspirations and equipping them to play an active and responsible part in improving the environment in which they live;

That they carry out school and out-of-school programmes designed to train women to cope more effectively with their household responsibilities and to foster their social, economic and cultural advancement.

The implementation of the lines of emphasis or guidelines contained in the recommendation necessitate a complex and extremely varied range of measures. Two of them call for special comment: the division of education into stages and the type and level of personnel needed to provide education in the rural environment.

In rural areas we must accept the principle, expressed in the recommendation, that the entire school-age population should complete primary education. In previous sections of this book, we have noted that a growing number of schools in the region are not providing the complete primary course. For many countries, one of the possible solutions, in terms of school organization, would be the general extension of one-teacher schools providing the complete primary course in scattered or isolated settlements where the size of the school register does not justify the services of more than one teacher, or where communication difficulties or economic constraints on the establishment of suitable transport services rule out the adoption of the formula applied in certain countries involving nuclear or district schools attended by children from different localities.

This type of school meets with a certain amount of opposition from some sectors of the teaching profession. The main objection is that it is difficult to teach groups of different ages and levels of attainment at the same time. This is certainly a difficult task if the teacher concerned has not been specially trained for work in a one-teacher school providing the complete course. In point of fact, it is rare to find in the region's teacher-training systems, or in-service teacher-training activities, any serious instruction or practical work geared to giving the teacher a proper training in this field. Some activities designed for this purpose were carried out within the framework of Unesco's major project on the extension of primary education. They were well received and brought about significant changes in a number of countries. This form of action seems to have been subsequently neglected, despite the fact that the problem has not been solved and that both economic and education considerations justify or demand this type of school. It is obvious that the one-teacher school caters for a heterogeneous body of pupils. However, heterogeneity is not merely a matter of age differences. It is found among any group of children, in the sense that they all have different learning abilities, ways of life and behaviour patterns. Furthermore, a well-organized one-teacher school, run by a suitably qualified teacher, provides a very good framework for individual learning, mutual help among the pupils and the development of personal initiative. All of these are recognized to be of unquestionable educational value.

Nevertheless, the training of young people in the rural areas involves requirements that cannot be met by primary or basic education alone. Many of these are better catered for by non-formal education. There are many instances of formal secondary education being able to make one of its stages in a way complete, providing a solid basis of education for everyday life, without excluding the possibility of access to further studies in subsequent stages of secondary and higher education. However this may be, formal secondary education must be supplemented by non-formal educational opportunities enabling those not attending school to acquire knowledge at this level.

Rather than considering post-primary or post-basic education as instruction suitable for a particular age-group, it should be regarded as providing a variety of types of education whose main aim is to prepare students for their future life. The requirements and practices of education should be geared to employment opportunities and living conditions. Obviously, this could be partially achieved by the formal education system, but a diversified out-of-school education system, rounding off school instruction, would have the most important role to play here.

To sum up, the creation of a system of educational networks enabling formal and non-formal education to be dovetailed, at all levels and in all their forms, with institutions and programmes closely linked with other services designed to promote community development would seem to be the most appropriate strategy for the specific conditions of the rural environment and the one most likely to bring about significant progress in extending and improving educational opportunities for rural populations.

As far as rural teachers are concerned, it is a well-known fact that they have not always received sufficient preparation to cope with the special demands of teaching in rural areas. Moreover, the isolation in which they often find themselves and the lack of available facilities and of professional and financial incentives offer them no encouragement to stay in such areas. In many cases, measures seem to be called for which would combine the following: (a) a complete overhaul of systems and methods of training for the future teacher with a view to bringing him into direct contact with real life in the rural areas where he may be called upon to practise his profession—this overhaul should not be confined to curricular content but should cover, as one of its vital components, teaching practice; (b) the development of in-service training schemes for personnel who have not been specifically prepared for the teaching profession so as to place them on the same level, in all respects, as those graduating from regular teaching education colleges; (c) the allocation of increased resources of a higher standard (teaching aids and equipment) and the provision of training for their use, and for turning to account the potential resources of the milieu; and (d) the setting up of forms of inter-school organization and communication which will help to end the isolation in which the rural teacher finds himself.

At times, the real opportunities for action by teachers in the rural environment have been exaggerated. The teacher has been expected to take on a complex variety of tasks and, consequently, to have an encyclopedic range of knowledge covering such areas as health, agriculture, co-operative schemes, light industries, etc.; in a word, he was expected to be the community leader. Such hopes were ill-founded: encyclopedic knowledge is usually superficial and often results in pedantry. The teacher certainly has a socio-cultural function, which he cannot perform properly without suitable training and a particular sensitivity. However, education in the rural environment involves more requirements than can be met by the professional activities of a teacher. The content of education and its relevance to the individual and collective needs of the inhabitants of rural areas can, however, be enhanced by using personnel from other sectors engaged in the promotion of rural development. In the rural environment, programmes of study should not be limited solely and exclusively to activities carried out by teachers. Many of them should be organized to allow for the joint participation of personnel from different sectors and of community leaders (agronomists, doctors, and specialists in nutrition, domestic science, co-operative schemes and the social sciences). Only such an interdisciplinary and inter-sectoral approach can ensure the success of rural development.

The marginal populations of urban areas

Familiar features of the outskirts of many of the cities of the region are overcrowding, an absence of basic public services, such as transport, electricity, drinking water or sanitation, and inadequate health, education and recreational facilities. All these factors, combined with the lack of employment opportunities and hence income, produce a situation of extreme poverty that is sometimes more acute than the poverty of the rural milieu from which these people came, where they were at least able to subsist by cultivating the land. The sprawling shanty-towns around São Paulo, the *favelas* of Rio de Janeiro, the *ranchos* of Caracas and the *chabolas* of a good many Latin American capitals in many cases present an appalling picture of subhuman living standards, which stands in dramatic contrast to the affluence and luxury enjoyed by other, more fortunate sectors of the population living a very short distance away.

The children and young people in these marginal populations are at an obvious disadvantage in comparison with the average urban schoolchild, even when, as is seldom the case, the same educational opportunities are provided for them. Many of them are forced to do jobs of all kinds in order to help the family survive; they lack the most elementary facilities to enable them to do the homework that school requires; the illiteracy or low level of instruction of the parents, particularly of the mother, deprives them of the understanding, encouragement and support that other groups of children enjoy in their school activities; their undernourishment, inadequate language development and insufficient ability to interpret a highly coded environment are, from the outset, fundamental disadvantages for them as regards their chances of educational success and, consequently, social advancement.

The countries in the region have, to a varying extent, made efforts to meet the educational needs of the marginal urban populations through formal and non-formal education programmes. As regards formal education, there has been an attempt to provide these groups with the same kind of primary or basic, secondary and vocational education as that traditionally designed for the urban middle classes, which seems reasonable in that it offers these populations the same educational opportunities as those enjoyed by other social groups in the urban environment.

However, two types of factors have combined to limit the effectiveness of these measures: first, the disadvantageous position of educational establishments situated in marginal areas as regards premises, teaching materials, the calibre of teaching staff, and transport and social welfare services for the pupils, and, second—and more important still, the difficulties experienced by children and adolescents from such areas in fitting into the prevailing education system and succeeding within it. This is reflected in the high rates of absenteeism, repeating of grades and dropping-out, and also backwardness in terms of the ages normally corresponding to the various grades and level of education.

This situation would seem to call for a review of aspects requiring special attention if the education needs of the marginal urban groups are to be met more effectively. In the first place, it must be recognized that policies are required which will cater for the needs of such groups on an integrated and co-ordinated basis, enabling education to achieve its own objectives and at the same time contribute to the success of activities carried out by other sectors in areas such as employment, housing, nutrition and health, recreation, sanitation and environmental improvement and community development. In the second place, mention must be made of the exceptional importance here of pre-primary education programmes, which enable children to be brought at an early age into an environment that is more favourable to their physical, biological, intellectual and social development, thus offsetting the adverse conditions of family and local community life. Although in general content and quality the education offered cannot differ from, or be inferior to, that provided to other urban groups, school organization and the methods used in the teaching and learning processes and in the evaluation of results should be adapted to the specific characteristics and particular needs of children and adolescents from these groups. Here, perhaps more than anywhere else, education must be problem-oriented and must lay emphasis on the development of knowledge, skills and activities that will equip individuals to improve their living conditions.

School principals, inspectors and teachers should, therefore, be trained to identify and comprehend the wide range of problems and difficulties faced by pupils in these marginal groups, and to increase contacts with their families and make the school a more inviting place, which will encourage pupils to stay on and succeed in their educational career. Their teachers should be trained not only to develop their academic and teaching capacities but also to be responsive to the nation's social problems and to those of the local community in which they work.

Education and the world of work

At the Mexico City Conference, two fundamental questions were raised in this connection, namely the relationship between education and employment, and the linking of education and productive work.

Education and employment

A previous chapter has drawn attention to the magnitude of the disparities between education and employment. In most countries today, whether developed or developing, this is one of the most serious problems, and one for which there is no short-term solution in view. The 15-to-24 age-group is the worst hit by unemployment. As a source of individual frustration and an underlying cause of growing social unrest, unemployment poses one of the greatest threats to peace and human well-being. The measures adopted in some countries to extend the duration of compulsory schooling seem to be dictated, in certain cases, by a concern to cushion or disguise the situation in regard to youth unemployment. However, this approach probably serves only to put off finding a real solution to the problem.

In his book, *Education and employment*,[1] Martin Carnoy considers the role which education can play in reducing unemployment. He distinguishes three broad categories of unemployed:

The large sector not integrated in the economically active urban population. This category embraces young people, workers from the least-privileged social classes, including the first generation of peasants settled in the urban environment, and a substantial number of women.

Mature skilled workers since, in the long run, the introduction of new production techniques and the reorganization of certain branches of industry represent a potential threat to their employment.

1. Martin Carnoy, *Education and Employment: A Critical Appraisal*, Paris, Unesco/IIEP, 1977. (Fundamentals of Educational Planning, 26.)

Young people who have received a higher education.

In some countries, these young people expect to find a job matching their degrees or diplomas. They run the risk of spending years in temporary jobs without any prospects while waiting for a permanent job in keeping with their qualifications.

Carnoy's description may be regarded as a fair picture of the situation in Latin America and the Caribbean. Each of the categories described calls, naturally, for different educational measures. It seems highly unlikely that the group of persons covered by the first category will enhance their employment prospects simply by improving their level of education if the average level of instruction of the economically active population rises at the same time: the improvement will serve only to give them a more complete education, not to create new jobs. A more constructive approach would appear to be to organize crash courses of occupational retraining for persons of suitable age and ability who have lost their jobs as a result of improvements and changes in the production system in certain industries.

The problem of the employment of graduates of institutions of higher education has given rise to two opposing positions which are reflected in the conditions for admission to education establishments at this level. The first position is stated very clearly by M. A. Prokofiev:[1]

Some colleagues from capitalist countries are anxious whether under this system the rights of man to an education are not infringed? Is it right, they usually ask, if 15,000 young people, say, want to study law, while you accept only 8,000? We shall reply to this question by another question: Do you think it right if the higher school graduates several thousand lawyers who are not able to find work in their line? Are not there enough tragedies of this kind in the capitalist world? Is it not more democratic to tell a young man to think of another speciality rather than to train him to be a 'superfluous' specialist?

The countries that follow this line of approach work to a programme or estimate of the number and type of professionals to be trained for a given period and take the view that the true democratization of education offers the assurance of finding a job at the end of the course of study. The advocates of the opposite point of view consider access to higher education a fundamental right and do not link it strictly to employment prospects.

In Latin America, in the early 1960s, attempts were made to carry out studies that would make it possible to forecast medium- and long-term manpower needs and translate those needs into terms of education and training. These attempts came up against a twofold constraint: the difficulties involved in determining the rate and structure of economic growth and the uncertainty of its variables, and the pressure of the demand for education, which exceeds the limits imposed by any pre-established formula attempting to match supply with the demand for skilled personnel at particular levels.

1. M. A. Prokofiev, 'The Soviet Higher School', in M. A. Prokofiev, M. G. Chilikin and S. I. Tulpanov, *Higher Education in the USSR*, p. 10, Paris, Unesco, 1961. (Educational Studies and Documents, 39.)

There is no doubt that the very considerable heterogeneity in technological terms which is a feature of all the main sectors of economic activity, as reflected, for example, in the disparity between craft or *minifundio* activities and the advanced technology used in certain industrial enterprises, poses serious problems for the planning of human resources in market economies. Furthermore, the economies of the region are affected by external economic factors, including technology, which can bring about substantial transformations in national economic processes. The combination of a restricted market with great occupational diversity and instability makes it hardly feasible—or at the very least difficult—to ensure that education is fully responsive to the immediate or expected requirements of the economy. These difficulties and the shortcomings of studies and forecasts of human resources conducted in the past are not, however, a reason for dispensing with them. On the contrary, there is an obvious need for efforts to re-activate them by adopting fresh approaches, so that they may provide guidance and support in decision-making and planning affecting systems of education and vocational training. It is essential to bear in mind that the developing countries need a far more flexible relationship between the structures of education and of employment than that existing in countries with comparatively stable economic and employment structures, lower population growth-rates and a certain established 'order' in the relationship between the education system and the world of work.

The conference clearly expressed its views on this problem when it recommended to the states of the region:

That they introduce into national education and development policies concrete measures to ensure an adequate link-up between the plans for the training of specialists at the middle and higher levels and the needs of the national economy;

That they encourage joint studies and projects between the bodies responsible for educational planning and those responsible for economic planning in Member States so as to facilitate the pooling of the means of ensuring close links between education and employment;

That they pay greater attention to the improvement of the methods used to plan technical and vocational education at the secondary and higher levels, gearing them closely to the advances being made in the techniques of economic and social development planning so as to achieve a more satisfactory harmonization of economic goals, those of employment and those assigned to the training of specialists, and to reduce the possible inconsistencies and distortions to a minimum.

The conference also advocated other measures, such as stimulating growth in sectors with the highest potential for generating employment, fostering vocational training for sectors where the demand is greatest, adapting the use of technologies to production processes (while bearing in mind the impact that this may have on employment), and promoting the introduction of accelerated vocational training programmes or open systems, with the aim of meeting the training needs of unemployed, underemployed and self-employed workers.

Education and productive work

In recent years a more general awareness has grown up of the need for education to be more closely connected with life, thus giving it more relevance to the needs of individuals and the requirements of national economic and social development. This concern is reflected in the introduction of a close link between education and productive work in the educational process. This relationship between education and the world of work is generally regarded as having three dimensions: (a) work as a fundamental part of the general education and the all-round training of children and young people; (b) education for work as preparation for a specific occupation, closely linked with vocational training, employment and manpower requirements; and (c) the association of education and work as part of the lifelong education of adults in order to assure the workers' right to education, and relating such education functionally to their work experience and the type of productive activity in which they are engaged. It should nevertheless be pointed out that these different dimensions of the relationship between education and work, given here in a very general form, assume different connotations according to the socio-economic context in which they occur.

The abolition of the division between intellectual and manual work is a constant theme in the thought of Karl Marx. It was undoubtedly inspired by a concern to overcome contempt for manual work, still encountered in many circles, and to accord it due importance and dignity. But, as we all know, abstract education still prevails, an education based on book-learning and reflecting a defective understanding of the nature of education, for it allows important faculties to atrophy. The ability to use one's hands for a wide variety of useful work is very important, as is the development of physical skills and abilities that are conducive to and complete any genuine education in the sense that they foster the all-round development of man. From the educational standpoint, the link between education and work fosters the practical application of theoretical knowledge, brings about a balanced development of the individual's intellectual and manual skills, and thereby helps to build up an all-round personality. Work experience brings the student face to face with real-life problems and situations, thus developing his ability to link knowledge with action, making him understand the importance of a job well done and familiarizing him with team-work and the sharing of responsibility.

Furthermore, it is considered that a link between education and work fosters an awareness of the dignity and value of work as a means of individual and social achievement. There are, moreover, obvious advantages in all students, regardless of social class, acquiring practical working experience and skills, for this is a way of averting the danger that education systems may encourage the development of hostile or largely unfavourable attitudes towards manual work and widen the social gap between the so-called intellectual and technical élites and the majority of the working population.

The conference recognized this when it drew attention to the necessity of teaching pupils from a very early age to appreciate the value of work and encouraging them to engage in work and productive activities through appropriate vocational guidance consistent with the physical and intellectual development of the child, while ensuring full compliance with national laws and the relevant international instruments, since the results produced will benefit the community, the school and the pupils themselves.

In this paragraph, mention is made of the extremely important yet more neglected activity known as 'vocational guidance'. Vocational guidance lends a deeply human dimension to what would otherwise be a strictly utilitarian exercise: matching the numbers and types of trained workers with the needs of the economy. The choice of a career involves taking into account the ability, aptitudes and inclinations of the individual, which are both fundamental to his job satisfaction and personal well-being and extremely relevant to his subsequent performance. This calls for observation and guidance throughout the pupil's course of study—a task considerably facilitated by the introduction of the wide range of activities involved in productive work—in order to determine as accurately as possible the areas in which the pupil is likely to succeed, and also to provide a careers information and advisory service to help the pupil in this vitally important task of choosing a career.

The idea of productive work in the context of general education is not confined to the organization of socially or economically useful activities. It embraces all intellectual, manual or artistic activity whose product is the result of the students' individual or collective efforts and is based on a combination of theory and practice, manual and intellectual skills. When seen from this angle, productive work can be arranged in a variety of ways and under many different circumstances: in school workshops and laboratories, in factories and during training periods in industry, on farms, by the local community services (hospitals, libraries, museums, etc.), in the maintenance, equipment and improvement of school premises and through participation in environmental preservation and improvement campaigns, and so on.

There are several ways in which general education and work can be linked and made complementary; initial experiments in this area have been undertaken in the countries in the region and, once evaluated and improved, they should be introduced on as wide a basis as possible. The foremost of these involves focusing scientific, social and arts subjects on various aspects of economic and social organization and the activities involved. Contacts between students and industrial firms or other centres of production and the various public services are being encouraged in order to familiarize students with the nature of the work they do, its processes and its products. These contacts enable professional people, technicians and workers to make their contribution to education and to enrich it with their experience of the different activities involved in the productive and service sectors.

Another approach takes the form of student participation during the academic year or vacation periods in community-development activities such as environmental preservation and improvement schemes, artistic activities, literacy and fundamental-education programmes, health services, housing and school-construction projects, etc.

Finally, there are instances of productive work being made a part of school activities. In such cases, the types of activity involved—which may consist of manual work, industrial or agricultural production, artistic creation or social work—are determined in the light of the specific contexts in which the schools operate. The work performed by students includes activities to raise funds for their school, the maintenance and improvement of premises, building and repairing of facilities, production of teaching materials, and so on. The general yardstick for selecting and evaluating such forms of work should be their educational value, their productivity and their social relevance and usefulness.

The important point is that productive work, whatever its type or form, should be an integral part of the whole teaching-learning process, serving both as a starting-point and as a meeting-point for the various school disciplines. If work experience is unrelated to the rest of the learning process, not only will education as a revitalizing force have failed to fulfil its purpose, but the learning process itself may be reduced to something purely mechanical, a series of activities which, for lack of any aim, may well be regarded as useless by students, teachers and the community alike.

In view of its nature and objectives, the introduction of work experience into the education process necessarily involves linking the school with the life of the community, with its institutions, social services, centres of production, natural resources, etc. The first reason for this is that it ensures that the work experience of the students, whether inside or outside the school building, is relevant to the real world of production and to the social and economic needs of the community of which the school is part. Second, it is the community, with its resources and production systems, which provides schools with the possibility of organizing socially useful work-experience activities for the students. Finally, the school needs the help of many different members of the community, whose experience in production and the social services will be invaluable in planning, organizing and developing students' work-experience activities.

Higher education, development and the democratization of education

Various themes relating to higher education have been considered indirectly by several of the conferences of ministers that Unesco has convened in the region, in particular by the Venezuela Conference held in 1971, but the fundamental problems at present encountered at this level of education were discussed in broader terms and in greater detail at the Mexico City Conference. In certain countries there is little contact between ministries of education and universities or equivalent institutions, due partly to the independence of the latter and, in some cases, to their politicization, and this hampers communication between them. This lack of contact has adverse repercussions on the education systems, which must be united and closely interrelated if they are to be efficient. Furthermore, the university, as the peak of the education system, has a responsibility towards the other levels of education and particularly towards teacher-education; it is clearly desirable that there should be such continuing contact between the highest level of education administration, represented by the ministries, and the governing bodies of institutions of higher education. The Mexico City Conference provided a useful opportunity to consider these questions, which will probably be the subject of future discussions.

The democratization of higher education

As we have seen in the chapter on quantitative advances in education systems, higher education has developed proportionately more than other levels of education. The rate of growth is higher than in the other regions of the world and double the world average.

This shows that there has been a substantial advance in the democratization of education, particularly in the case of women, whose enrolments in higher education rose from 29 per cent in 1960 to 42.1 in 1977.

Together with this significant increase in the number of enrolments, the number of institutions of higher education has grown considerably. In 1976/77 there were some 450 establishments at that level in the countries of the region, although their numbers vary appreciably from country to country. The rapid growth in the number of such establishments has been particularly marked since 1970. In Mexico there were fifty-one universities in the 1976/77 academic year[1] and 121 other institutions of higher education (technical, vocational, teacher-training and general education), giving a total of 172 institutions of higher education. In Venezuela, there were seventeen universities in the same period. The increase is due not only to the high enrolment ratios but also to the establishment in recent years of a considerable number of smaller institutions providing only a few courses and indeed sometimes only one.

This increase in the number of institutions is not always accompanied by decentralization. Higher education establishments are often concentrated in metropolitan areas and the main urban centres; in some countries, more than half the total enrolments are in the capital. Besides this, universities vary considerably in size; some of them have between 1,000 and 3,000 students, while others are very large; the University of Havana, the University of Zulia in Venezuela, the National University of Córdoba in Argentina, and the Central University of Ecuador all have about 50,000 students. The National University of Buenos Aires and the Autonomous National University of Mexico are in a separate category, each having enrolment figures of around 200,000. Higher education has also expanded rapidly in countries that have gained their independence more recently, for instance in Suriname, in the West Indies where the university has three campuses (at Mona in Jamaica, St Augustine in Trinidad and Cave Hill in Barbados), and in Guyana, which founded its own university in 1963.

The very swift growth in the number of private universities, which now make up 54 per cent of the total number, is largely due to the great demand for higher education. Many of these private universities are small, and they usually concentrate on providing the traditional courses, for which teaching costs are low. In some cases their standards in the matter of infrastructural requirements and academic levels are not very high. It should be emphasized, however, that the standard of private establishments of higher education varies considerably: some have an established reputation, which is well deserved; others are of doubtful quality.

Such rapid expansion in higher education raises a number of questions, in particular the question of the extent to which it has produced a student body of more diversified social origins, by providing a juster and fairer system of access; the question of the effects of such 'massification' on the quality of education; and, lastly, the question of employment prospects for the many university graduates.

In a paper presented at a seminar held in Bogotá,[2] Germán Rama, the

1. *International Handbook of Universities and other Institutions of Higher Education*, 7th ed., London, published by MacMillan for the International Association of Universities, 1977.
2. Germán W. Rama, *Condicionantes sociales de la expansión y segmentación de los sistemas universitarios*, Buenos Aires, 1980 (mimeo).

co-ordinator of the Unesco/ECLA/UNDP Project on Development and Education in Latin America and the Caribbean, considered the first point: the social origins of students. He analysed the problem as follows.

Various factors help to perpetuate the preponderance of the upper social groups in total enrolments. Among the most significant of these factors are the following:

(a) Between 1950 and 1975, female enrolments increased steadily until they nearly caught up with male enrolments, except in the majority of the Andean countries (Bolivia, Colombia, Ecuador and Peru), Mexico and the Central American and Caribbean countries, in which women account for between one quarter and one third of total enrolments.

   A large proportion of the new female students come from families who already sent their sons to the university. Furthermore, in the first stage of the increase in female enrolments, female students inevitably came from higher social groups than male students, since the modernization of the female role began in the upper-middle and upper social groups.

(b) Part of the increase in enrolments was due to the fact that a greater area was covered. The establishment of provincial universities gave educational opportunities to upper-middle social groups who were formerly less inclined to send their children to a university than their counterparts in the capital cities, because of the additional expense involved in attending the university in the capital and also because they wished to avoid breaking up the family.

(c) The increase in university enrolments was paralleled by a rise in the number of tertiary occupations, so that analyses of stratification by the father's occupation do not show significant changes in the origins of the students.

The children of peasants still do not go to the university. More of the sons and daughters of working-class people now attend universities than in the past, and the growth rates for this class are high, but as the initial enrolment figures were extremely low the high growth rates do not mean that there are large numbers of working-class students. The greatest increase is in different groups belonging to the lower middle classes, particularly the children of office workers, lower managerial staff, tradespeople and self-employed workers in the modern services.

   The increase in the number of university students from the non-manual middle-level occupational strata is accompanied by progressive internal stratification in these groups, which takes the form of differences in income and social position, but is also associated with marked dissimilarities of cultural background.

   When not offset by a satisfactory primary and secondary education, the low cultural level of the emergent groups acts as a barrier, since the members of these groups are lacking in the kind of cultural background which the upper social groups have and which is needed for a university education. The result is that, although significant opportunities for access have become available, as a rule they have only led to the sort of course and levels of knowledge which will enable the persons concerned to maintain the same social position as their parents had.

'Massification' and quality

There is widespread concern about the adverse effect of the 'massification' of higher education on its quality. This point is a bone of contention between those who advocate very wide access to higher education and those who take the view that education at this level necessarily requires that prospective students have a certain intellectual ability. In the words of the eminent scientist Julian

Huxley, who was the first Director-General of Unesco and who could hardly be suspected of cultural Malthusianism:

Those who can profit by working for a university degree constitute only a proportion of the population, whether the proportion be 20 or 40 or even 60 per cent: for the remainder to attempt it is waste of their own youth, of the time and talents of university teachers, and of public money.

The discussions at the Mexico City Conference showed that people were concerned about the poor quality of higher education resulting from 'massification'. It was argued that there was a tendency towards the lowering of academic standards and the fragmentation of the higher-education subsystem to the detriment of its quality, which resulted in differences in employment opportunities and levels of remuneration, thus tending to perpetuate social inequalities rather than to eliminate them.

It was noted that the number of institutions—particularly private institutions—is increasing rapidly and in most cases without adequate planning, either as a response to social demand or as a result of prestige considerations leading to the unwarranted upgrading of institutions whose standard is poor, or to the establishment of new ones which have not sufficient resources to ensure their academic quality. Many such institutions are smaller than the minimum critical size, their academic organization is incomplete and they do not offer a full range of studies. At the same time, excellent new higher-education institutions have been established, and older institutions have been considerably improved, so that there are variations in the quality of education and the value of diplomas. It is considered essential to take steps to ensure that the democratization of education does not impede the maintenance of a high quality of education and the value of diplomas.

The quality of education is undoubtedly affected by the frequent conflicts resulting from the politicization of the university. This is a sensitive issue, but it must not be evaded. The conference acknowledged that little attention had been given to the question, and expressed the view that such conflicts seemed to be linked with the frustration arising from disparities between the cultural mobility afforded by university-level studies and the growing difficulty of achieving the goals of social and economic advancement. The politicization of the university is an indisputable fact; a university is a place of political discussion, which sometimes leads to internal conflict or external clashes. Universities are attended by idealistic young people, and it is natural and understandable that students should protest against social injustices or abuses of political power and react against them forcefully. The propriety of political agitation and unrest in education institutions is more questionable, and they are less justified in countries where normal channels exist for dealing with political and social problems, mainly because they hamper the real functions of the university, which are to foster learning, transmit knowledge and train efficient workers for the professions.

Dissatisfaction with the efficiency of the university has led to a call for far-reaching reforms, and in fact many have already been embarked upon or carried through, in the hope of solving the difficult problem of reconciling the traditional functions of universities with the new tasks of education at university level and of striking a proper balance between the humanistic role of education at that level and specialized training requirements. Those planning reforms should draw their inspiration from the role of higher education and its responsibility for promoting democratization and social integration, endogenous development, and social and cultural progress. Content and subject-matter need to be changed, and courses must be reorganized so that they are more problem-oriented and more interdisciplinary. Education, training and research should be more closely related to national goals and objectives, both long and short term, as well as to national and local conditions and requirements. This often calls for co-operation with local authorities and the productive sector, as well as for sectoral planning within overall development plans at both national and regional level.

The employment of university graduates

Unemployment among university graduates is extremely widespread today. This problem exists in Latin America as much as anywhere else, although in the last few decades the increase in the number of employees required in the service sector has created a wide range of job opportunities for university graduates. The state, which establishes social services and administrative and other official posts, has contributed to this increase in no small measure. None the less, the signs are that this increase will not continue, and the trend may even decline. One reason is that business concerns are reluctant to take on graduates with no work experience and, as the public sector has generally employed young persons in recent years, it is not likely that their posts will become vacant for some considerable time. The fact that university students are only too well aware of the grim employment prospects contributes significantly to social malaise and unrest.

This situation, combined with the uncontrolled increase in the number of public and private universities, makes it necessary to plan the development of higher education organically, so as to avoid the establishment of new institutions, which is in many cases unjustified, as well as the surplus of graduates in certain fields.

The solution of this problem will depend on nationwide educational planning such as will ensure that a rational approach is made to the setting up of new units, that their location is more carefully chosen and that there is equal opportunity of access to higher education in keeping with the real needs of the population in each country by making maximum use of the academic resources available. In the course of the past decade, various universities in the region have been endeavouring to introduce planning processes designed to ensure the coherent development of higher education in line with the requirements of national development, to establish a closer relationship between the educational, financial and administrative spheres and to encourage the participation of the different groups forming the university community. In many countries, a national system for co-ordinating higher education institutions has been introduced, either on the initiative of the institutions themselves or by government bodies. New legislation concerning the universities has accordingly been drawn up, and numerous national higher-education associations and bodies responsible for the co-ordinated development of education at that level have been set up or strengthened. In some countries these associations or boards of rectors have been accorded official status and placed in the category of public bodies entrusted with the task of planning the organic development of higher education.

At the Mexico City Conference, the Regional Centre for Higher Education in Latin America and the Caribbean was entrusted with the task of undertaking an 'investigation of the occupational tasks performed by professional persons with university qualifications in order to determine what type of knowledge is necessary for production and high-quality performances'; and it was suggested that 'special attention should be paid to those situations in which scientific and technological knowledge is a basis for innovations in the production process and also to the identification of the way in which additional knowledge, over and above stipulated requirements, is conducive to an improvement in production and in the organization of society'. The objectives set out in the Mexico City Convention[1] should also be taken into account.

The university and research in the service of development

If higher education is to contribute to development greater attention must be paid to science and technology education at the higher level, as regards both the percentage of students—a point referred to above—and the importance attached to research. For a long time universities were basically oriented towards education and training, and undertook little or no scientific research. Although some pioneering experiments were conducted, it was only in relatively recent years that higher-education institutions began to introduce scientific and technological research activities on any significant scale. Many countries still need to make a sustained effort in this direction.

Many of the region's universities still have a poor record as regards the training of high-level scientists. There is, however, no doubt that the greatest potential for scientific research in terms of human resources is to be found in the universities, and it is due mainly to their contribution that, in some countries, the number of scientists and technicians working in research and technological development has increased in the last few decades.

If a country is to achieve cultural as well as economic independence and

1. Regional Convention on the Recognition of Studies, Diplomas and Degrees in Higher Education in Latin America and the Caribbean, signed by the states of the region, under the auspices of Unesco, Mexico City, 19 July 1974.

free itself from dependence on other countries, a greater effort must be made to develop scientific and technical research and training. The social and human sciences should also be developed, since they perform the important function of humanizing the process of development and defining its goals and aims. The gradual disappearance of social scientists and of social science training centres from many Latin American universities and countries is a serious problem.

But the trouble is that socio-economic development in the region often relies on scientific and technological skills from abroad and does not encourage the full employment of the scientific and technical manpower resources of the region. This is one reason why many highly qualified specialists emigrate, thus creating a serious problem from the point of view of the use of human resources and also from that of the endogenous development of the countries in the region. The conference therefore made a recommendation to the Director-General of Unesco that a study be undertaken that will indicate to Member States how to ensure the retention of high-level specialists in their countries of origin by fostering methods that will bring home to them the needs of their own country and the importance of their role in the latter's development, and that he consider ways and means of guaranteeing adequate conditions of employment and of actively opposing the exodus of specialists, persons with professional qualifications and researchers.

Higher-education institutions in the region are becoming increasingly aware of the need to encourage basic research in relation to national development and its problems, for it is now generally accepted that progress in applied research depends on the advances made in basic research. Accordingly, more applied research programmes are being focused on studies which will contribute to socio-economic development and particularly to the medium- and long-term planning of such development.

None the less, under present circumstances it will be very difficult for the universities to make any significant or effective response to the demands of scientific and technological development, except in the few cases where they have sufficient resources to do so. This situation partially explains the emergence of other national scientific and technological research bodies. Under these circumstances, there is a vital need for the co-ordination of research activities between the universities themselves and also with the activities of other establishments of the type mentioned above. This clearly shows the need for scientific and technological development plans that are based on national priorities, and designed to ensure the coherence and complementarity of research work and its multisectoral and interdisciplinary character. Such plans will enable higher-education institutions to select subjects for research work more judiciously and to justify their requests for more funds to be allocated to research.

The conference accordingly recommended that Member States should study ways and means of assigning national priorities to the research problems to be tackled in the medium term, and of defining the need for co-ordination among institutions performing such research with the aim of promoting co-operation, the utilization of scientific information and the exchange of the results obtained, and that they set up interdisciplinary science and technology information centres and data banks.

It must be pointed out that the contribution of research and higher education to development should not be planned on the basis of purely economic considerations. Social and cultural development is as important as economic and technological development, and both should ultimately be concerned with man, who is both the focal point and the agent of development.

At the same time, the interrelations between the different types of education and the training based on the various disciplines and areas should be strengthened. There are at least three reasons for this. First, since the ultimate aim of technological progress is to foster social advancement and the full development of man, science education is essentially closely related to human and social science studies at the higher level. Moreover, this conception of development is perfectly in keeping with the region's humanist tradition. Second, the development which many Member States of the region are endeavouring to bring about is endogenous development, designed to promote solutions which are consistent with the particular conditions of these countries, which reflect their own genius and historical background, and which help to eradicate any remaining dependence on outside factors. Science is not neutral: it transmits cultural values, and its applications change people's way of life, social structures and even a country's culture, so that the contribution of the social and human sciences and that of the natural sciences must both play their part. Third, there are some contemporary problems which demand an interdisciplinary approach that in itself reflects the complexity of situations, and which also call for various types of functional training of an interdisciplinary kind from which specialists can obtain the particular theoretical and practical information they need for the effective performance of their tasks. Environmental problems are an example of this, for they must be understood by a large number of professional personnel (other than ecologists themselves) who are responsible for such fields as administration, planning, engineering, town-planning, architecture and medicine.

Lastly, if the university is to contribute to development it must co-operate with those responsible for planning economic and social development and for the different sectors of production, such as firms, industrial and agricultural complexes, trade unions, and so on.

The responsibility of higher education towards the education system

The education system is an organic whole. Higher education is favourably or adversely affected by the quality of the preceding stages of education, and the converse is even more true, particularly in view of the role generally played by the university in teacher-education. Furthermore, because the university is the summit of the education system, it has a great responsibility of an essentially technical nature, which it shares with educational management. But in fact relations between the different levels of education are characterized more by a lack of contact than by co-operation.

The university can perform a most useful function in relation to the other levels of education in a number of ways: (a) by playing its part in the preparation and application of educational reforms; (b) by participating in general reflection on the objectives of education, as regards both national development and the full development of the individual; (c) by conducting the necessary research in the various educational sciences; and (d) by assuming responsibility for the training of the different categories of educational personnel required for the establishment of comprehensive, diversified systems which meet the requirements of lifelong education.

The linking of school and out-of-school education in the context of lifelong education

The Mexico City Declaration states that

uninterrupted development and progress in all fields of knowledge, and especially in science and technology, and economic and social transformations require that education systems be designed and operate within the context of lifelong education, that a close relationship be established between school and out-of-school education and that appropriate use be made of the scope offered by the mass media.

The massive emergence of the modern communications media, particularly in the last three decades, has suddenly brought about a spectacular increase in the supply of information which has manifold repercussions, the scope and prospects it offers for education being among the most important. Some educators see the communications media as a somewhat disruptive competitor, or rival, of formal education; others have overestimated the ability of the new media, thinking that they could replace educational institutions as we know them today. Obviously, the best thing to do is to combine the two forms of education. The interest shown in these media, particularly radio and television, and their almost spell-binding effect on children and adults make them extremely valuable instruments, as long as the content of the information they transmit is what it should be. Furthermore, they reach the most isolated and remote areas where, in some cases, educational institutions cannot easily be established.

School and out-of-school education systems, therefore, should not be regarded as mutually exclusive alternatives, or as competing with each other from the point of view of value and importance, priorities and resources; for each has its own essential function, and the two are complementary and have common aims: to satisfy the right of everybody to education and to contribute to the development of society. Because of their common aims, school and out-of-school education should be co-ordinated, both in national education policy-making and planning and in the structuring and organization of educational processes; and they are also the basic criteria to be used in deciding—while taking account of the educational and socio-economic characteristics of each country—what functions each of the two subsystems should perform, how they should complement each other and what machinery should be set up for this purpose.

A recent study by Cole S. Brembeck[1] examines the influence that such linkages may have on education for change and on preparation for the world of work:

Initiating and implementing change are two quite different activities and they call for the application of different means. For example, formal education may be best suited to conceptualizing and planning change; non-formal education seems best suited for implementing change. Formal education incorporates change agents, such as teachers trained in cosmopolitan centres, a systematic way of inquiring into subjects and organizing knowledge, and a tradition of research. Non-formal education, on the other hand, is geared to action and the application of knowledge. When the goals are both the initiation and implementation of development change, a wise course would seem to be an association of the two in a sequence beginning in knowledge generation, conceptualization and planning, and ending in application, work and action.

Agricultural development is an example. Many breakthroughs in the plant and animal sciences have come out of university laboratories and experimental stations. In themselves these breakthroughs cannot increase agricultural production. Beyond the formal system, and linked to it, there needs to be a non-formal system which operates through extension programmes. It is this linking system that can penetrate the infrastructure of agriculture to reach the farmers and revolutionize agricultural production....

A second area in which efforts to achieve a better fit may be observed is that of preparing for the world of occupations.... Many vocational and technical education programmes are unrelated to the world of work and isolated in schools. They are frequently ineffective. The reason may be that a formal school, detached from the world of work where knowledge is put to use, is simply a poor choice of educational means. Could it be that these programmes are better linked to the work place, where students would be assigned to do a job for portions of each day?[2]

Lifelong education offers the most suitable framework for achieving such linkage; and in this connection the specific functions of school and out-of-school education must be made clear, for both have their part to play. As we know, lifelong education is really a broader interpretation of the right to education, which should be available to everybody according to his age, his needs and aspirations and the work he does, throughout his life. The formal education system, at least as it is today, performs the important function of providing humanistic training of a literary, scientific and technological nature. It is a limited function, however, for two reasons: because it is confined to certain ages and because it requires full-time study. Out-of-school education is intended for people of all ages who are outside the formal system and who, for the most part, are involved in the active world of social participation and work. Consequently, most of them, unlike the children and young people still in the

---

1. C. S. Brembeck, 'Linkages between Formal and Non-formal Education', *Educational Documentation and Information: Bulletin of the International Bureau of Education* (Geneva), Nos. 212/213, 3rd/4th Quarter 1979.
2. Ibid., pp. 11–12.

formal system, need education directly connected with the social activity they are carrying out or that they wish to carry out in the immediate future; if they wish to acquire more knowledge, it is not out of interest in the subjects of study as such, or a desire to apply their knowledge later on, but because they want to improve their present living and working conditions. This being so, only a comprehensive system of education, comprising both school and out-of-school structures, and in which the forms and levels of education are correlated and complement one another, can meet the twofold need for education that continues throughout people's lives and that is also closely connected with the real world of the needs of individuals and of society. The scope for lifelong education in the region is virtually boundless.

The Argentine educationist, Gilda de Romero Brest, in her paper for the Unesco Symposium on the Contribution of Persons other than Teachers to Educational Activities,[1] lists the following functions of lifelong education:

The updating of capacities, ideas, attitudes in various spheres because new circumstances have arisen; retraining (occupational, political, etc.) following the modification of occupations; specialization for specific, practical tasks (professional, family, cultural); the broadening and diversification of scope of perception, information, comprehension, action; training in specific 'know-how' for concrete activities (work, use of communication media, free time); encouragement, mobilization of efforts, for full participation in decisions, programming and evaluation of public, socio-cultural and political matters; promotion towards advanced forms of knowledge, interpretation of reality, innovation, creation.

The educational situation in most countries of the region is such that out-of-school education programmes will have to be developed in order to compensate for the fact that large numbers of both the urban and the rural population have little opportunity to obtain a general basic education and preparation for the world of work and, because they have had little or no education, are always poor and take little part in the life of society. In so far as out-of-school education aims at this objective and attains it, its programmes should be given priority in the distribution of resources, since it is of direct benefit to the cultural, social and economic development of the different countries.

Another vulnerable sector of society in Latin America and the Caribbean is made up of unemployed young people who have no political, economic or social responsibilities and who, consequently, have no opportunity to fulfil their proper role in society. In view of the standard of school education in the region, and in particular the high drop-out rates in the short term, there can be no hope of preparing all young people for occupational, social and cultural life by means of school education alone. This is particularly true of young people in rural areas and the marginalized urban populations, whose feelings of frustration at the lack of opportunities to participate are most marked.

1. Gilda L. de Romero Brest, *Some Points for Reflection Proposed by the Participants*, pp. 23–7, Paris, Unesco, 1976 (doc. ED-76/CONF.811/4). Paper presented at the Symposium on the Contribution of Persons other than Teachers to Educational Activities in the Perspective of Lifelong Education, held at Unesco Headquarters, Paris, 13–17 September 1976.

There is a great variety of forms of out-of-school education, many of which are already being implemented in the region. They include initial and pre-primary education programmes, some of which include intersectoral activities in: child-rearing, health and nutrition; programmes of diversified distance education; open summer schools; schools providing complementary instruction; special education programmes; literacy campaigns for young people and adults; people's education centres; education programmes to promote citizenship and community organization; school amenity building programmes; education programmes for adults in a rural environment designed to improve health conditions, provide information on legislation, contribute to rural community organization, improve productivity and promote and disseminate culture.

The conference echoed the extremely widespread desire for out-of-school education courses or activities to be legally recognized. To this end, it recommended that Unesco undertake a study whose aim will be to seek ways and means of enhancing the status of out-of-school education at every level and in all its forms, in harmony with education in the formal system, so as to confer social, economic, educational and occupational recognition on studies pursued in an out-of-school context.

Linking school and out-of-school education poses difficult problems which those responsible for education policies, planning and administration will have to solve: problems relating to legislation, intersectoral co-ordination, administrative responsibilities and hierarchical relations; the conditions governing entrance upon courses and their completion; the question of compulsory attendance; arrangements for alternating periods of education and work; the reform of curricula and of systems for the training of teachers and administrators; the preparation of multi-purpose teaching materials; the design and use of school premises; the combination of traditional learning methods with the way in which the modern mass media can be used, and so on.

While it is important to establish and strengthen machinery to facilitate such linking, it is even more important that interdisciplinary institutions or groups be set up to study and evolve alternative ways and methods of establishing complementary relations between school and out-of-school education. All the countries in the region are equipped with centres for research, educational development and the development of curricula and teaching materials, which, if strengthened and redirected, could carry out this new and complex task of examining and advising on changes to be made or measures to be adopted in order to co-ordinate educational structures, the organization of teaching and learning processes, programmes of study, procedures for the evaluation, admission and promotion of students, education legislation, and so on. Linking two education systems, each of which has its own philosophy and both of which are designed to work separately, will be difficult. Considerable thought, research and study will be needed if the decisions that are adopted concerning the link-up are to work and really further the end in view.

The countries of the region are already trying out ways of linking school and out-of-school education. These highly important but limited experiments should be encouraged, stepped up and extended. Of particular importance and rich in innovative potential are all the efforts deployed to link technical, vocational and general education with productive work, to establish equivalences of studies and facilitate the flow of students between the two subsystems, and to set up centres whose infrastructures and staff may be used for both school and out-of-school education programmes. Other ways in which the two kinds of education are being linked consist in: the establishment of open education systems based on self-teaching; the development of tele-education programmes from which both school pupils and those participating in non-formal programmes may benefit; the preparation and dissemination of teaching materials which are suitable for both school and out-of-school education; and the participation in adult-education programmes of teachers from the school-education system.

One of the main contributions to the linking of school and out-of-school education will have to be made by education personnel themselves. As their role changes with the changes occurring in education systems, and particularly as the idea of lifelong education is put into effect, new policies for the initial and in-service training of such personnel will have to be worked out, and the traditional training systems will have to be altered to suit the new requirements. In the context of lifelong education, initial training will be merely a first step in a teacher's professional development; in-service training will become indispensable, since the qualifications required will be periodically redefined according to the changes being made in the education system. Moreover, the establishment of the flexible and versatile structures that the linking of school and out-of-school education necessitates will also create a need for all-round teacher-training.

Co-operation for educational development and the new international order

Background

From the chapter on education trends in Latin America, as seen through the regional conferences of ministers of education, one can get some idea of the influence exerted by Unesco on a theoretical level and through its various practical achievements such as the Major Project on the extension and improvement of primary education in Latin America. While this is hardly the place to give a detailed account of Unesco's co-operation in the region over the years, the following concise list will show the extent of its action in the field of education. At the regional level, assistance has been given to institutions such as the Regional Centre for Adult Education and Functional Literacy (CREFAL), the Latin American Institute for Education Communication (ILCE) and the Regional School Building Centre for Latin America and the Caribbean (CONESCAL), and to regional, subregional or national co-operation programmes implemented with the support of UNDP, in conjunction with the World Bank, the Inter-American Development Bank and Unicef. Co-operation with ECLA has also been strengthened with a view to carrying out various studies and projects, and the co-ordination of activities with the OAS has been improved.

In the last decade, Unesco has provided technical co-operation for 109 projects in 29 countries in the fields of planning, administration and supervision, initial and/or in-service training for teachers, technical and vocational education, rural education and integrated education programmes. A smaller number of projects, implemented in a few countries, dealt with other matters such as population education, agricultural education, the curriculum, primary education and research. Lastly, an even smaller number of projects concerned the more specific topics of evaluation, secondary education, science education, special education, university education and the use of radio.

The UNDP-assisted projects cover practically all areas of education, all levels of the system and all forms of education. Those funded by the World

Bank are concerned with agricultural secondary education, science education, technical education, rural education and the strengthening of the institutional structures of ministries of education. The projects funded by UNFPA are concerned with different aspects of population education. Finally, projects in receipt of contributions from Trust Funds promote the development of basic education, technical education, vocational training and non-formal education.

The Regional Office for Education, based in Santiago, performs the following functions:

It provides training and further training for basic education and secondary-school teachers and for specialists in educational planning and administration and other aspects of education.

It advises governments on the formulation and implementation of their education plans.

It prepares conferences of ministers of education convened by Unesco in the region and co-operates in the application of their conclusions and recommendations.

It provides technical support for Unesco projects and experts in the region.

It provides information and documentation services for ministries of education, teacher-training establishments and education research centres.

It conducts studies and research on education trends and problems in the region.

A co-ordinator, who is the representative of the Director-General of Unesco throughout the region and for all the programmes within the sphere of competence of the Organization, is based in Caracas, where the Regional Centre for Higher Education in Latin America and the Caribbean (CRESALC) has also been established.

In the discussions at the conference, many speakers praised the effective way in which the regional and international agencies had co-operated with the countries in activities for promoting, expanding and improving education since the Caraballeda Conference in 1971. The contribution that Unesco had made, both at headquarters level and through units operating in the region, was considered satisfactory, and the increasing trend towards greater decentralization of operations was noted with approval.

Special mention was made of certain aspects of Unesco's co-operation in the region. Speakers expressed appreciation of the way in which some countries were conducting operational activities for which Unesco was acting as executing agency, carrying out, in conjunction with the governments concerned, projects financed by UNDP, the United Nations Fund for Population Activities (UNFPA), the Inter-American Development Bank, the World Bank and other funding sources. Some delegates observed that the technical support which Unesco had provided when their countries were reforming their education systems or programmes was of considerable importance and value. The collaboration of the Regional Office for Education in this type of activity and in the implementation of Unesco's general programme in the region was considered to be very valuable.

In addition to giving their views on the way in which national projects and
co-operation activities were being carried out, the delegates referred to the
growing interest shown in subregional and regional projects in which groups of
countries co-operate with Unesco and UNDP. The results achieved by the
Network of Educational Systems for Development in Central America and
Panama (the RED project) were praised and the establishment of the Central
American Educational Co-ordination System was singled out as an illustration of the importance of supplementing external co-operation by using
mechanisms agreed upon by the countries themselves. Several speakers
considered that the recent establishment of the Unesco Office for Regional
Co-ordination in Caracas, Venezuela, and of the Office of the Unesco
Representative for the Caribbean in Kingston, Jamaica, was a most desirable
contribution to concerted intersectoral action and decentralization.

However, a number of criticisms and reservations were expressed on the
subject of external co-operation. The importance of better co-ordination was
stressed, and it was observed that, since the development of education was the
responsibility of states, every effort should be made to ensure that when
international co-operation was to be combined with national activities
questions of timing, scope and procedure should be decided by the national
authorities. The risk of any form of external imposition must be avoided. The
role of National Commissions for Unesco in co-ordinating national plans with
the resources of the international community was emphasized by some
delegates, while others stressed the fact that no effort should be spared to
ensure that activities receiving technical and financial assistance from various
external sources were properly co-ordinated.

Emphasis was placed on the need to review the methods used for selecting
experts and integrating their advisory activities into national plans and
institutions, so as to ensure that the cost of technical co-operation would be
more satisfactorily related to its results and that national technicians would
play a greater part in projects being carried out in their own countries. It was
thought desirable that Unesco's units in the region should be strengthened,
especially in regard to their human and technical resources. In particular, it
was stressed that Regional Offices should be assigned greater responsibilities,
for which they would require greater resources, as part of a general
decentralization policy on the part of Unesco.

Future action

From the resolutions of the conference it is clear that the three fundamental
aims that should inspire and guide subregional, regional and international co-
operation are regional integration, the new international economic order and
endogenous development.

The long-cherished aim of Latin American integration, clearly
formulated by Bolívar at the Congress of Panama, is becoming increasingly
regarded by the peoples of the region as a prerequisite for the assertion of their

personality and influence in a world context and the stimulation of their own development.

There are indications that progress is being made towards this goal; the stage of pronouncements is being superseded by that of action to give effect to the principles and aspirations of integration. In recent years subregional bodies have been set up with political or economic aims which are evidence of the will to co-operate. In the field of education, various important agreements for the same purpose have been signed: the Andrés Bello Convention concerning educational, scientific and cultural integration, signed in Bogotá by Bolivia, Chile, Colombia, Ecuador, Peru and Venezuela; and the Central American Agreement on Co-operation in Education, the Arts, Science and Technology, with its predecessor, the Central American Agreement on the basic unification of education and the establishment of the Department of Education of the Caribbean Community. These achievements are an indication of the prospects for regional co-operation.

As far as education and culture are concerned, a full-scale blueprint for integration already exists. The contribution made by international co-operation, particularly by Unesco, to the extension and strengthening of the education programmes being developed by the above-mentioned bodies augurs well for regional integration.

Such an effort could be particularly beneficial to endogenous development if there is effective regional co-operation; experience of international aid shows that aid is doubly effective when donors and recipients are countries possessing the same cultural milieu.

An endogenous effort to achieve scientific and technological development is one of the principal ways to eradicate the relations of dependence which often threaten a nation's future. Only if they develop their own scientific and technological capacities will the nations of the region (and the region as a whole) be able to obtain for themselves the knowledge needed to ensure their material development, by means they have freely selected, at the same time preserving their own freedom.

Such development is seen by the countries of the region as part of a new international economic order based, according to the Declaration adopted by the United Nations in 1974, on equity, sovereign equality, interdependence, common interest and co-operation among all states, irrespective of their economic and social systems, which shall correct inequalities and redress existing injustices, make it possible to eliminate the widening gap between the developed and the developing countries and ensure steadily accelerating economic and social development and peace and justice for present and future generations.

In *Moving towards Change*[1] the Director-General of Unesco, Amadou-Mahtar M'Bow, speaks of the contribution of the Organization to the new international economic order in the following terms:

1. *Moving towards Change: Some Thoughts on the New International Economic Order*, Paris, Unesco, 1976.

Unesco's task in particular will be: to contribute to the laying of the scientific and technological foundations which will enable every country to make better use of its natural resources; to broaden the scope of education and direct its course so that the people of each country will be better fitted to see to their own development; to develop communications and information systems; and, through the development of the social sciences, to stimulate self-examination in every society in order to help it to derive the greatest advantage from the instruments of change, whilst not losing its own identity.

The General Conference of Unesco, in resolution 100 adopted at its nineteenth session, reaffirmed this broad concept of the new international economic order, from which social, educational and cultural dimensions are inseparable.

Forms of action

The different sections of this publication have dealt with problems, objectives and priorities in education. The main fields for external co-operation must be in accordance with the national plan of each country, its problems, aims and priorities. However, experience of such co-operation, with its successes and its failures, indicates that the procedures used for co-operation should be modified considerably.

First, we must think of co-operation in a different way from in the past; indeed a beginning has been made in this direction. We should not regard it as a form of assistance rendered by a superior to an inferior, but as a collaborative task whose results are beneficial to all the parties involved; that is to say, co-operation should be a means of promoting solidarity, integration and joint progress, while preserving the cultural identity of the countries involved.

Advocating the renewal of methods and forms of action, the conference singled out the following as being particularly suited to Unesco's co-operation: (a) decentralization, while ensuring the continuation of the process of establishing the Organization more firmly, by strengthening Unesco's Regional Offices for Education, Science, Technology and Culture, with the human, material and financial resources that will enable them to broaden the scope of their respective activities; (b) the setting up of a permanent subregional office with the Unesco Representative in Central America and Panama to facilitate communication between the subregion and Unesco and to ensure stronger co-operation in the subregional, national and local projects and activities of the countries concerned; (c) the study of the most appropriate possibilities and machinery for the establishment of an Office of the Unesco Representative for the countries of the Andean Group; and (d) the reinforcement of existing offices of Unesco representatives, especially the Kingston office, which serves the Caribbean subregion. The strengthening of the functions of, and the stepping-up of contacts between, the National Commissions of Unesco, which are a suitable means of liaison, information and implementation, within the scope of each state, of the programmes drawn up by, or relating to, the Organization, in which the governments of the region participate, as well as consulting them more frequently and effectively, with a view to ensuring that the Organization's programmes cater adequately for the education priorities of the Member States.

The conference recommended:

That, within the Draft Programme and Budget for 1981–1983, provision be made for appropriate negotiations with funding organizations that will lead to the financing of a horizontal technical co-operation programme among the countries of Latin America and the Caribbean, at the bilateral, subregional or regional levels.

That in the implementation of this programme use be made preferably of units from outside the Headquarters of the Secretariat; that the Director-General of Unesco convey to the Secretary-General of the United Nations the Conference's wish that the Intergovernmental Committee on Science and Technology for Development, whose creation was approved at the Vienna Conference, be established and assume its functions as soon as possible, taking due account of Unesco's valuable institutional collaboration as the international agency best suited to develop programmes in this important field.

That the project concerning the Regional Co-operative Network for Educational Innovation for Development in Latin America and the Caribbean be implemented.

Education for the future:
the new Major Project

When Unesco's activities in Latin America are reviewed and assessed, there is general agreement that the Major Project on Education implemented between 1957 and 1966 was one of the most valuable activities carried out in the region and one which had the greatest multiplier effect. Its clearly defined objectives were intended to solve what the countries themselves saw as priority problems at that time. The fact that it was designed and implemented at regional level, with the participation of all the countries of the region, constituted both a source of encouragement and a step forward towards new forms of co-operation. The experiments conducted at the pilot centres, such as the Associated Normal Schools, made a real and effective contribution to the reform of teacher-training curricula. The associated universities, together with ILPES, which worked in conjunction with the Educational Planning Section of Unesco, trained the personnel who were to assume important roles in the renewal of education systems and educational administration. One of the achievements of the project was that it encouraged a spirit of emulation in national efforts to attain such lofty aims as the general observance of the right to education—and education of a high standard—and combined such national activities with regional and international co-operation. Without losing sight of the link with Unesco and operating at all times under the supervision of Unesco Headquarters, the Major Project was essentially a decentralized, regional undertaking, planned and implemented in such a way as to ensure the complete autonomy of those it served.

The Major Project has been unsurpassed as a means of bringing together and pooling efforts. While it was regional in scope, a number of isolated projects were undertaken which lacked the mutual benefit to be derived from the systematic exchange of ideas and experiences on common objectives as well as from the evaluation of their results such as was periodically conducted by the Advisory Committee of the Major Project. This committee was composed of twelve countries of the region, serving in rotation, and the Project Co-ordination Office. One of the advantages of the latter was the constant mobility of its personnel, particularly the travelling experts, who at all times played their part in national activities—courses, seminars, advisory work—connected with the project activities.

It is hardly surprising, therefore, that in view of the widespread conviction that the Major Project had been planned and implemented along the right lines, those attending the Mexico City Conference expressed the hope that a new major project would be undertaken which would attempt to solve the problems confronting education in the latter part of the twentieth century, and meet the desire to raise the standard of education and stimulate scientific and economic development, as an essential means of bringing about a more prosperous and just society, a society that will benefit all men without distinction and will preserve and enhance respect for distinctive cultures and traditions.

The countries of the region, in co-operation with Unesco, will have to decide upon the nature and the main lines of emphasis of the new Major Project, which will embody the fundamental features of the Mexico City Declaration as set forth in it. The following considerations are intended merely as brief and, of course, personal reflections on this subject, and are accompanied by some principles which might be adopted in the complex task of planning the new project.

In planning the project, attention to the problems of today should be combined with that forward-looking view, always necessary in any educational endeavour, which essentially must prepare for the future. As regards the future, we should do well to remember that the beginning of the twenty-first century is already in sight and must be borne in mind in planning the education of those who are now starting school and whose lives will be led in the next century.

On the basis of these facts and of the main points made in the Mexico City Declaration, the project might be planned as follows:

Its main goal would be to raise the standard of education and science in Latin America and the Caribbean and, in particular, to eliminate adult illiteracy and low school-enrolment rates in the case of children.

It would be an interdisciplinary project, embracing educational, scientific, cultural and communicational activities.

It would be a regional project, involving the participation of the countries of the region, of Unesco (mainly through its competent regional offices and centres) and of regional and subregional bodies.

In preparing its national plans, each country should set itself realistic objectives in keeping with its level of educational and socio-economic development, and should translate them into goals that can be achieved gradually over a three- or five-year period.

Objectives of the project

The project must have the following objectives:

The provision of a general education of at least eight to ten years' duration and the inclusion in the system of all children of school age before 1999, in accordance with national education policies.

The elimination of illiteracy by the end of the century and the extension of education services for adults, particularly the least-privileged groups of the population in rural areas and the outlying districts of cities.

The improvement of the efficiency and quality of education systems, especially through teacher-training and research and the combination of school and out-of-school education.

Contribution to scientific, technological and cultural development and to the development of the communications media by improving the formal and non-formal education systems.

The reform of educational administration and the training of educational management personnel.

Bibliography

AVANZINI, Guy. *Immobilisme et novation dans l'éducation scolaire.* Toulouse, Privat, 1975.
Boletín of the Unesco Regional Office for Education in Latin America and the Caribbean (OREALC), Santiago de Chile.
Boletín demográfico de CELADE (Santiago de Chile, Centro Latinoamericano de Demografía), Vol. XII, No. 23.
CARNOY, Martin. *Education and Employment. A Critical Appraisal.* Paris, Unesco/IIEP, 1977. (Fundamentals of Educational Planning, 26.)
CIRIGLIANO, Gustavo, F. J. *Universidad y pueblo.* Buenos Aires, Librería del Colegio, 1973.
Curricula and Lifelong Education. Paris, Unesco, 1981. (Education on the Move, 1.)
Final reports of the international conferences on education. Geneva, Unesco/IBE, 1975, 1977, 1979.
Final reports of the regional conferences of ministers organized by Unesco since 1956.
ILLICH, I. *Deschooling Society.* New York, Harper & Row, 1971.
Informe de la Comisión de Evaluación del Proyecto Principal sobre Extensión y Mejoramiento de la Educación Primaria en América Latina. Santiago de Chile, February 1966.
International Handbook of Universities and Other Institutions of Higher Education. 7th ed. London, Macmillan Press, for the International Association of Universities, 1977.
La primera década del programa regional de desarrollo educativo PREDE-OEA y sus perspectivas y planes futuros. (Document prepared by the General Secretariat of the Organization of American States.)
La situación educativa en América Latina; la enseñanza primaria: estado, problemas, perspectivas. Paris, Unesco, 1960. 295 pp.
LEMKE, Donald. *La investigación educacional en Latinoamérica y el Caribe: una visión histórica.* Santiago de Chile, Unesco Regional Office for Education in Latin America and the Caribbean, 1975. 24 pp.
Long-Range Policy Planning in Education. Paris, Organization for Economic Cooperation and Development (OECD), 1973. 391 pp.
MÁRQUEZ, Angel Diego. *Educación comparada; teoría y metodología.* Buenos Aires, Librería 'El Ateneo' Editorial, 1972. (Series: Nuevas orientaciones de la educación.)
MIALARET, Gaston (ed.). *The Child's Right to Education.* Paris, Unesco, 1979.

MORALES GÓMEZ, Daniel A. (comp.). *Educación y desarrollo dependiente en América Latina.* Mexico City, Ediciones Gernika, 1979.

Moving Towards Change; Some Thoughts on the New International Economic Order. Paris, Unesco, 1976.

PAZ, Octavio. A Matter of Life and Death; Aztec Myths and Christian Beliefs in Mexico. *Unesco Courier* (Paris), August/September 1977, pp. 21, 24 and 26–7.

PIAGET, Jean. *Science of Education and the Psychology of the Child.* London, Longman, 1971.

Problemas y tendencias de la administración educacional en América Latina y el Caribe. Santiago de Chile, Unesco Regional Office for Education in Latin America and the Caribbean, 1977. 202 pp.

Prospects—Quarterly Review of Education. Paris, Unesco.

Publications of the Project for Development and Education in Latin America and the Caribbean (UNESCO-ECLA-UNDP), in particular: *Expansión educational y estratificación social en América Latina, (1960–1970),* by Carlos FILGUEIRA, 13 September 1977, 124 pp. (summary in English) (doc. DEALC/4); and *Educación para el desarrollo rural en América Latina,* by Abner PRADA, 15 June 1978, 51 pp. (summary in English) (doc. DEALC/11.)

RAMA, Germán W. *Condicionantes sociales de la expansión y segmentación de los sistemas universitarios.* Buenos Aires, 1980. (Mimeo.)

REGIONAL CONFERENCE OF MINISTERS OF EDUCATION AND THOSE RESPONSIBLE FOR ECONOMIC PLANNING OF MEMBER STATES IN LATIN AMERICA AND THE CARIBBEAN, MEXICO CITY, 4–13 DECEMBER 1979. Documents prepared by the Unesco Secretariat: *Quantitative Evolution Projections of Enrolment in the Educational Systems of Latin America and the Caribbean. Statistical Analysis* (ED-79/MINEDLAC/Ref. 2); *Education in the Context of Development in Latin America and the Caribbean* (ED-79/MINEDLAC/3); *Unesco's Activities in the Field of Education in Latin America and the Caribbean Region since the Conference Held in Caraballeda in 1971* (ED-79/MINEDLAC/Ref. 3). Document prepared by the United Nations Economic Commission for Latin America (ECLA): *Structure and Dynamics of Development in Latin America and the Caribbean and their Implications for Education* (ED-79/MINEDLAC/Ref. 1).

REIMER, Everett. *School is Dead.* Harmondsworth, Penguin Books, 1971.

SYMPOSIUM ON THE CONTRIBUTION OF PERSONS OTHER THAN TEACHERS TO EDUCATIONAL ACTIVITIES IN THE PERSPECTIVE OF LIFE-LONG EDUCATION, UNESCO HEADQUARTERS, PARIS, 13–17 SEPTEMBER 1976. *Some Points for Reflection Proposed by the Participants,* pp. 23–7 (Paper by Gilda L. de Romero Brest). Paris, Unesco, 1976 (Doc. ED-76/CONF.811/4).

TORRES BODET, Jaime. *Discursos, 1941–1964.* Mexico City, Editorial Porrúa, 1965.

Unesco Statistical Yearbook, 1977. Paris, 1978. 1064 pp.

VASCONI, Tomás A.; RECA, Inés. *Modernización y crisis de la Universidad Latinoamericana.* Santiago de Chile, Facultad de Ciencias Económicas de la Universidad de Chile, 1971.